THE UNIVERSITY OF MICHIGAN
CENTER FOR CHINESE STUDIES

MICHIGAN PAPERS IN CHINESE STUDIES

Ann Arbor, Michigan

The Economy of Communist China
1949-1969

With a Bibliography of Selected
Materials on Chinese Economic
Development

Chu-yuan Cheng
Department of Economics, Lawrence University
formerly
Senior Research Economist
Center for Chinese Studies
The University of Michigan

Michigan Papers in Chinese Studies
No. 9
1971

Open access edition funded by the National Endowment for the Humanities/ Andrew W. Mellon Foundation Humanities Open Book Program.

Printed and bound by CPI Group (UK) Ltd, Croydon, CR0 4YY

ISBN 978-0-89264-009-6 (hardcover)
ISBN 978-0-472-03839-8 (paper)
ISBN 978-0-472-12820-4 (ebook)
ISBN 978-0-472-90220-0 (open access)

Table of Contents

The Economy of Communist China, 1949-1969

Economic development in mainland China during the first
two decades of Communist control provides a typical example for the
difficult task to transform a vast underdeveloped agrarian economy
into a modern industrial one. In the first half of this period, a series
of massive transformations of social and economic institutions was
accompanied by a drafted industrialization program; the result was
an impressive speed-up in economic growth. The second decade
witnessed an economic crisis (1960-62) and a political upheaval
(1966-68). These disruptions marred the economic performance over
the period as a whole. Consequently, the long-term growth rate appears
to have been only moderate.

Any study of the economic development of the first twenty
years in Communist China is greatly complicated by the paucity of
reliable data and the contradictions in the Communist Chinese official
reports. However, with careful examination and comparison, one can
still draw some general conclusions.

The purpose of this paper is to review selected aspects
of the economy. I shall first of all examine the development strategy
and then analyze the quantitative trends and the structural changes.
Subsequently, I shall analyze the key factors contributing to the earlier
growth and the elements responsible for the later disruption. The
final section will provide an assessment of the impact of the Cultural
Revolution on the Chinese economy and the prospects of the current
Third Five-Year Plan.

Since this is designed to be a comprehensive survey, most
of the discussions will be general and brief, in order to bring out the
major trends.

1

(I) <u>The Changes in Development Strategy</u>

When the Chinese Communists assumed power in October 1949, they inherited an economy that can be called backward by any quantitative criterion. Prolonged external war and subsequent civil strife had inflicted immeasurable damage. Confronting this situation, the new government set forth two major economic goals: first, to restore the deteriorated economy as soon as possible, and second, to begin a rapid, forced-draft industrialization program to break the vicious cycle of backwardness and poverty.

In the course of industrialization, the economy experienced acute imbalances, strains, and supply bottlenecks, which forced the planners to alter their scheme. In terms of scale of priority, rate of capital formation, and investment technique, the development strategies followed between 1949 and 1969 can be roughly divided into four consecutive stages.

<u>The Unbalanced Growth Strategy, 1949-57</u>

During the early years of the industrialization program, the Chinese development strategy almost completely duplicated the Soviet model.[1] The features of this strategy consist of (1) a high rate of capital formation, with overwhelming emphasis on industrial development; (2) a high priority on the expansion of the capital goods industry; and (3) a preference for larger plants and for capital-intensive techniques. During China's First Five-Year Plan (1952-57), the ratio of gross investment to gross domestic product in terms of 1952 constant prices was about 20 percent, compared with only 6 percent in the prewar period. Of the investment in capital construction, 48 percent was concentrated in industry, of which 85 percent was for heavy industry.[2] Since agriculture provided the lion's share of total savings, the essence of this development policy was simply a continuous squeeze of the agricultural sector to support heavy industry.

In the choice of technique and scale, the Chinese planners also followed the Soviets, by investing in relatively large and capital-intensive projects. More than 85 percent of the capital investment was allocated for the 694 large industrial projects, leaving only 15 percent for the more than 10,000 small projects.

The Soviet model proved to be quite successful in the early stage of China's industrialization. The capacity of major industry expanded rapidly. According to official statistics, gross domestic product grew at an annual rate of 8.9 percent and industrial production at 18 percent.[3] The growth of agriculture, however, lagged far behind that of industry. During the same period, agriculture rose 4.5 percent a year and output of food grains by 3.7 percent, barely surpassing the population growth rate.

As a result of the deliberately unbalanced growth strategy, the growth soon hit its ceiling. In 1956, a sharp increase in capital investment over the preceding year immediately caused inflationary pressures on the commodity market. Bottlenecks in materials and transportation and difficulties in the balance of payments forced the planners to reduce the rate of investment. In the following year, investment slipped back 7.4 percent and the growth rate was curtailed. This retrenchment caused underutilization of industrial capacity and a rapid rise in unemployment. The applicability of the Soviet model to China was questioned by economists and top planners.[4] A new approach to economic development was planned by the Chinese leaders in late 1957, and a new drive, know as the Great Leap Forward, was introduced in 1958.

The Great Leap Forward, 1958-60

The general idea behind the new strategy was to accelerate simultaneously the growth of both the modern and the traditional sectors. Although capital goods industries were still accorded high priority, agriculture was no longer neglected. The strategy thus shifted from concentration of investment in a few lines to a more balanced pattern. Such a shift required a larger investment to push the ceiling upward. The new idea was to substitute labor for capital or to use surplus labor for capital formation.[5] The concept came very close to Ragnar Nurkse's proposal, which also focused on labor absorption or employment-generating effects of industrialization.[6]

Large-scale water conservation projects involving 100 million peasants were undertaken in late 1957 and early 1958.[7] Next, a more drastic drive to build millions of small plants and mines using indigenous methods of production was carried out in the whole country. Some sixty million persons were mobilized in the so-called "backyard blast furnace" drive.[8] The new strategy not only eliminated all surplus labor but also created a critical shortage of manpower in the agricultural sector. This led to the establishment of the rural commune as a means of releasing peasant housewives from household chores to participate in productive activities.[9]

In the first year of the Great Leap, both industrial and agri-cultural output rose sharply, partly because of the exceptionally favorable weather in 1958 and partly because of the establishment of millions of small plants.[10] In general, Nurkse's capital-creation approach seemed to be gaining ground in the Chinese case.

However, the exuberant phase was short-lived and illusory. Most of the small workshops and backyard furnaces, lacking technical equipment and skilled labor, turned out unusable products at exceed-ingly high costs, while the commune system destroyed peasant incentives and caused mismanagement of agricultural production. The economy's limit of tolerance was soon reached and the new drive lost its momentum. Agricultural output, affected by both adverse weather and manmade mistakes, dropped precipitously in 1960,[11] and industrial output went down subsequently. The new strategy, instead of moving the economy ahead, brought it to the brink of a total collapse.

The Adjustments, 1961-65

In order to alleviate the mounting crisis, the strategy of development was drastically revised. A new policy of "readjustment" (of the pace of development), "consolidation" (of existing plants), "reinforcement" (of the weak links), and "improvement" (of quality of products) was implemented in 1961.[12] The scale of capital investment in industry was sharply reduced. Agriculture received first priority, followed by light and heavy industry in descending order.[13] Most of the small workshops erected in the Great Leap period were abandoned. Employment in the industrial sector was appreciably curtailed. During 1960-61, some twenty million workers and urban dwellers were sent back to the countryside to reinforce the agricultural front.[14] Industrial investment was concentrated in those branches which could support the agricultural sector, notably chemical fertilizers and agricultural machinery. The new strategy thus represented a complete reversal of the "unbalanced growth" of the first period and also differed materially from the labor-absorp-tion strategy of the second period.

To stimulate workers and peasants, material incentives were reemphasized. The commune system underwent a complete revision.[15] Private plots of land were redistributed to individual peasants, and farm markets were reopened to provide a channel for private exchange. A nation-wide increase in salaries and wages was made in 1963. As a result of these revisions, agricultural output began a slow recovery. In 1964, grain output slightly surpassed the 1957 level.[16] By 1965, most of the industrial output has attained the 1958-59 level. The Chinese economy as a whole had recovered most of the losses caused by the Great Leap.

The Modified Great Leap Scheme, 1966-

The stress on material incentives caused widespread "capitalist tendencies" in the rural areas, which signaled the general favoring of a revisionist line like that prevailing in the Soviet Union. Toward the end of 1965, on the eve of the new Third Five-Year Plan, debates on the new lines of economic development erupted in the top hierarchy of the Communist Party. Those leaders in charge of Party affairs and economic planning apparently favored a continuing relaxation. They argued that industrialization could only be achieved by economic means. Material incentives and profits were both indispensable for running the economy, regardless of the differences in social structure. They opposed mass participation in economic construction and were convinced that industrialization required the guidance of experts, factory directors, engineers, and technicians. Their views, which underlay the adjustments of 1961-1965, were the antithesis of the views advanced by Mao Tse-tung, the author of the Great Leap and the communes.[17]

According to Mao and his followers, if China followed in the footsteps of the West and the USSR, she would encounter numerous bottlenecks in capital supply and technology. Her economy would then grow at a snail's pace. Instead, China should adopt a spartan type of economy wherein political indoctrination would replace material incentives. Once properly indoctrinated and committed, the immense manpower of China could become a source of tremendous energy which could bring about a high rate of economic growth.[18]

The schism between these two views together with other conflicts finally developed into the fierce power struggle known as the Great Cultural Revolution. During this period, many radical measures similar to those of the Great Leap were resurrected. Material incentives were condemned as "economism." Mass participation in industrial management was encouraged. College-trained engineers and technicians were downgraded. Small-scale plants were again in favor. [19] Although agriculture still was accorded the top priority, a large portion of capital investment was allocated to the nuclear program.

The vicissitudes of Chinese development strategy during the first two decades reflected a series of problems confronting the Chinese Communist leadership.

First, unlike in the Soviet Union, the capacity of the agricultural sector to support industrialization was rather limited in China. Over the entire period, there was keen competition for the scarce resources needed by both agricultural and industrial development. The change of priorities from the "heavy industry first" of the First Five-Year Plan period to "agriculture first" after 1961 clearly reflected the small tolerance of Chinese agriculture for being squeezed in support of industry.

Second, in the course of its industrialization the Soviet Union benefited substantially from the importation of modern science and technology, while Communist China was forced to pursue a technique of dualism - developing simultaneously a modern, large-scale, capital-intensive sector and a traditional, small-scale, labor-intensive sector. The amount of unemployed or underemployed labor in China was so immense and the capital-absorption capacity of modern technology so limited that China simply could not afford the same capital-intensive technique as the Soviet Union.

Third, although both Chinese and Soviet leaders infused economic behavior with ideology, the Chinese leaders apparently viewed it as an effective substitute for the scarce capital and backward technology. The ideological ingredient was never so strong in molding economic decisions in the Soviet Union as it was in Communist China during the past two decades.

(II) The Quantitative Trends of Output

Over the past twenty years the economy has gone through
a series of cyclical fluctuations marked by several peaks and troughs.
Domestic output grew in a fairly steady manner between 1950 and 1957.
It surged sharply upward in 1958-59 and then dropped steeply in
subsequent years. A slow recovery started in 1963, gained momentum
in 1965, and reached a new peak in 1966. The upward trend was
suddenly disrupted by the Cultural Revolution. By the middle of
1969, the economic situation in China was only slightly better than
that in 1966.

The Over-all Growth Rate

According to official statistics, China's net domestic product
rose 53 percent between 1952 and 1957, with an average annual growth
rate of 9 percent. In the two years of the Great Leap, net domestic
product rose by 34 percent in 1958 and 21 percent in 1959. [20]
Although in early 1960 the government did publish some preliminary
figures for 1960's economic plan, no final accounting has been made
public. Since 1961, the government has published practically no
economic indicators. It is therefore extremely difficult to make even
rough estimates of the growth rate in the later years.

Even for the 1952-59 period, official national income statistics are believed by economists outside China to embody some upward
biases because of three factors. First, the official data on agricultural production for the earlier years understated the actual
output because of incomplete coverage. As a result, the average
annual growth rates for the subsequent years were unduly inflated.
Second, because of the overpricing of industrial products, particularly capital goods, and the underpricing of agricultural and handicraft
products, official statistics also understated the weight of the slow-
growing sectors in the total product and hence overstated the aggregate
growth rate. Third, Communist national income accounts omit the
service sector, which grew at a much lower rate than the material
production sectors. This omission also tended to inflate the over-all
rate of growth. [21]

To remedy some of these defects, several attempts have been made by economists in the United States to construct independent estimates. [22] A widely accepted estimate was made by T. C. Liu of Cornell and K. C. Yeh of the Rand Corporation: they estimate the over-all average annual rate of growth during 1952-57 at only 6 percent, about 3 percentage points lower than the official statistics. [23] For the 1952-59 period as a whole, the Liu-Yeh estimate gives an average annual rate of growth at only 8 percent (Table 1).

Even though the Liu-Yeh estimate heavily deflates the official account, an annual growth rate of 8 percent is still very impressive. It outstripped most countries in the post-war period and was comparable to West Germany (7. 8 percent) and Japan (8. 8 percent) during the 1950's.

China's economy suffered a series of setbacks after 1961. For almost seven years (1969-65), the economy went through a cycle of recession and recovery with virtually no growth. The upswing started in 1963, reached a new high in 1966, and fell sharply in 1967 as a result of the unprecedented political turmoil. Taking the entire period into account, the long-term growth rate between 1949 and 1969 may range from 4 to 5 percent, appreciably lower than that in 1952-59.

Table 1

National Income Estimates, 1949–59

	(I) Official estimates		(II) Reconstructed Communist estimates		(III) Liu-Yeh estimates	
	Absolute amount[1] (billion yuan) (in 1952 prices)	Growth rate (%)	Absolute amount[2] (billion yuan)	Growth rate (%)	Absolute amount[3] (billion yuan)	Growth rate (%)
1949	35.69					
50	42.33	18.6				
51	49.53	17.0				
52	60.58	22.3	68.55		71.41	
53	69.08	14.0	73.27		75.33	
54	73.05	5.7	77.81		79.28	
55	77.80	6.5	83.34		82.30	
56	88.70	14.0	96.41		92.08	
57	92.78	4.6	104.22		95.34	
57	(in 1957 prices) 95.00					
58	127.30	34.0	144.97	39.1	108.0	13.0
59	154.70	21.5	176.75	21.9	125.0	15.7

Table 1 (contd.)

	Official estimates	Reconstructed Communist estimates	Liu-Yeh estimates
average annual growth rate[4]			
1949-59	15.8	n.a.	n.a.
1952-57	9.0	8.8	6.0
1952-59	14.3	14.5	8.0

Notes and Sources of Table 1:

1. Derived from Ten Great Years, p. 20; Yang Po, "The Relation Between Accumulation and Consumption in the National Income of Our Country, " in Hsin-hua Pan Yueh-kan (New China Semi-Monthly), No. 22 (1958); and Li Fu-chun, "Report on the Draft of the National Economic Plan for 1960, " Chi-hua yu T'ung-chi (Planning and Statistics), No. 4 (1960).

2. This estimate was reconstructed according to the standard Western concept without corrections of basic communist data. For figures of 1952-57, see Liu-Yeh, op. cit. , p. 213. For figures of 1958-59, see Ibid. , p. 660.

3. Liu-Yeh, op. cit. , pp. 66 and 660.

4. These are the simple arithmetic averages of the annual rates of change.

Growth of Industrial Output

A most spectacular economic performance in the 1949-68 period occurred in industrial production. According to official statistics, industrial output grew at 18 percent a year during 1952-57 and reached as high as 66 percent and 39 percent in 1958 and 1959 respectively. [24]

Like the statistics on national income, official gross output value of industry is also known to be a defective measure of achievement. First, the official gross value data was collected by the "factory reporting method," in which the grand total is simply the sum of the gross value reported by the individual enterprises. A change in vertical integration would automatically change the grand total even though the physical quantity produced remained unchanged. Second, industrial output was valued in constant 1952 prices, which overstated the value of producer good in relation to consumer goods. [25] Since output of the first group increased much faster than the second, the overpricing of the former put an upward bias into the official data. Finally, official prices also overvalued most of the new products, which usually grew faster than industrial output as a whole. Their overpricing introduced another upward bias.

Attempts at correcting these biases have been made by several scholars in the United States. Kang Chao of the University of Wisconsin has compiled an index of Chinese industrial output. His findings give annual growth rates of 14 percent for the 1952 period and 23.7 percent for 1949-59 (Table 2). Regardless of whether the official series or Chao's index is used, industrial development between 1952-59 must be rated as exceptionally rapid. Factory output almost doubled between 1952 and 1957, and nearly quadrupled between 1952 and 1959. This trend was sharply disrupted in 1961. Since then, official data for industrial output have been as scarce as other indicators. Based on fragmentary official data, I have constructed an index of industrial gross output covering 1957-66. [27] This index is based on official statements without correction for their biases. It is definitely inflated, because of the exaggeration of achievements during 1958-60, the period of the Great Leap.

An independent estimate was made by Robert M. Field of the
U. S. Government. Using estimates of physical output for ten major
industrial products, Field computed an output index with 1956 as the
base year. If we convert it for a 1957 base, Field's output index for
1965 would be about 25 percent lower than my index. While Field's
estimates are considered to be reasonable for the 1958-60 period,
his estimates for output performance after 1960 are suspected of
having over-corrected the official data and embodying a certain degree
of downward bias. [28] Since there is no way to determine the degree
of upward and downward biases in the two indexes, one convenient
expedient would be to compute an arithmatic mean of them based on
the assumption that the real growth rate fell between those two poles.
The result is shown in Table 3. It becomes clear that the long-term
growth rate in Chinese industrial production was much less favorable
than the short-term growth rate. For the period 1952-66 the growth
rate was in the neighborhood of 11 percent. Even so, the pace of
advance in industry is still rather impressive.

Agricultural Production

In contrast to the advance in industry, there was near stagnation in the agricultural sector. In the First Plan period, when
industrial output registered a 128 percent increase, agricultural
output grew by 24.7 percent, representing an annual growth rate of
4.5 percent. Output of food grains grew by 20 percent, with an annual
growth rate of 3.7 percent. Since the population grew at 2.2 percent
annually, the availability of foodstuffs rose at an average rate of
1.5 percent a year.

Even such low figures are considered by economists in this
field as dubiously reliable because of the incomplete crop reporting
in the earlier years, which leads to an exaggeration of the growth
rate over the entire period. The lack of substantial improvement in
agricultural production was clearly reflected in the persistent food
shortages in the urban areas, which led to the institution of a strict
rationing system after 1953. Stagnation in agriculture also hampered
the growth of the consumer goods industry, whose raw materials came
mainly from agricultural products. Toward the end of the First
Five-Year Plan, the textile and food processing industries operated
substantially below capacity, [29] because of the bottleneck in material
supplies.

Table 2

Industrial Production Indexes, 1949–59

(1952=100)

	(1) Official gross output value index[1] (factory & handicraft)	(2) Chao's gross output value index[1] (factory & handicraft)	(3) Liu–Yeh value- added index[2] (factory only)
1949	40.8	50.0	
50	55.7	63.3	
51	76.8	81.2	
52	100.0	100.0	100
53	130.2	122.1	122.9
54	151.4	139.4	142.2
55	159.8	149.7	159.0
56	205.0	179.4	210.8
57	228.3	189.8	238.6
58	379.4	251.5	289.2
59	528.6	330.9	373.5
Average annual rate of growth 1952–57	18.0	14.4	19.4
1952–59	26.9	20.6	21.1
1949–59	29.2	23.7	n.a.

Table 2 (contd.)

Sources:

1. Kang Chao, The Rate and Pattern of Industrial Growth in Communist China (Ann Arbor: University of Michigan Press, 1965), pp. 88, V 92.

2. Liu-Yeh, op. cit., pp. 146, 157.

Table 3

Indexes of Gross Industrial Output Value
1957-66

	(1) Cheng's index[1]	(2) Field's output index[2]	(3) Arithmetic mean of (1) and (2)
1957	100	100	100
58	166	157	162
59	231	199	215
60	298	296	252
61	149	136	143
62	134	120	127
63	168	132	150
64	193	148	171
65	214	161	188
66	256	195	226

Average annual rate of growth

1957-66	11%	7.7%	9.5%
1952-66	13.4%[3]	8.6%[4]	11.3%[5]

Sources and notes:

1. Chu-yuan Cheng, Machine-Building Industry in Communist China (Forthcoming), Chapter 6.

2. Robert M. Field, "Chinese Communist Industrial Production," in An Economic Profile of Mainland China, p. 273. Field's indexes use 1956 as the base. The 1956 base was converted to a 1957 base. Field's index did not include 1966. The 1966 figure was added by the author at the same rate of growth as official data.

3. The 1952-66 annual growth rate was derived by combining my index with the official index for 1952-57. Taking 1952 as 100, the 1966 index number is 584, representing an annual rate of 13.4.

4. The 1952-66 annual rate was derived by changing Field's index from 1956 to 1952 base and adding the 1966 official rate to his index. Taking 1952 as 100, the 1966 index number is 315, with an annual average growth rate of 8.6%.

5. The arithmetic mean for 1966 is 449.5, representing an annual rate of 11.3%.

Note: Field has revised his earlier estimate upward. It is, however, too late to use his latest estimate in this analysis. For details see Field, "Industrial Production in Communist China, 1957-1968", The China Quarterly, Apr-June, 1970, pp. 46-64.

It was against this background that a series of dramatic measures were introduced in 1958 to break the agricultural bottleneck. Many labor-intensive projects, such as water conservation, closer planting, and deep-plowing, were launched in the countryside on an unprecedented scale. In the zeal of the Great Leap, the regime put forward a set of very ambitious targets to raise the output of food grains and cotton by nearly 100 percent in a single year. [30] Despite repeated official claims of having fulfilled this fantastic plan, the country's agriculture in fact suffered its deepest crisis since 1949, because of mismanagement, numerous technical blunders, and three consecutive years of natural calamities between 1959 and 1961. Although agricultural output did rise 10 or 15 percent in 1958, when the weather was favorable, it dropped 25 or 30 percent in 1960-61 and pushed the country to the brink of a large-scale famine. Slow recovery started in 1962. By 1964, foodgrain output was only at the 1958 level. Small gains were recorded for 1965 and 1966. Exceptionally favorable weather brought about a bumper harvest in 1967, but in the following year output declined again. In terms of per capita food grain availability, the 1968 figure was the same as that of 1955; in other words, on a per capita basis, Chinese grain production during the past thriteen years achieved no growth at all (Table 4).

Other major farm products showed almost the same pattern. During the First Plan period, output of cotton rose from 1.3 million tons in 1952 to 1.65 million tons in 1957, an increase of 25.8 percent. Official claims for 1958 and 1959 were 2.1 million tons and 2.4 million tons respectively. Independent estimates, however, give 1.9 million tons and 1.8 million tons for these two years. Production dropped to about 1.55 million tons in 1960, and 1.45 million tons in 1961. A recovery started in 1962. By 1964, the output level was officially reported as only slightly higher than 1957. It is plausible to assume that the 1964 output of cotton might have been around 1.9 million tons, the same level as the estimated output of 1958. [31] There was no material change in cotton output in 1965 and 1966. Official sources gave a 10 percent increase in cotton output for 1967. This would put the output at 2.2 million tons, or 30 percent higher than in 1957.

During the 1962-64 period, much of the increase in agricultural production came from side-line products of the peasants. [32] The income from side-line occupations has become one of the main sources of rural income. [33]

Table 4

Production and Per Capita Availability of Foodgrains, 1952-68

Year	Foodgrain output (million tons)	Exports(-) or imports(+) (million tons)	Total availability of foodgrains (million tons)	Population (million persons)	Foodgrains per capita (kg.)
1952	154 [1]		154	569 [11]	270
53	157 [1]	-1 [8]	156	581 [11]	269
54	161 [1]	-1 [8]	160	595 [11]	270
55	175 [1]	-1 [8]	174	608 [11]	286
56	183 [1]	-1 [8]	182	621 [11]	293
57	185 [1]	-1 [8]	184	635 [11]	290
58	200 [2]	-1 [8]	199	645 [12]	308
59	175 [2]		175	655 [12]	267
60	150 [3]	+1 [8]	151	665 [12]	227
61	162 [3]	+5 [8]	167	675 [12]	248
62	174 [3]	+5 [8]	179	685 [12]	261
63	183 [3]	+5 [8]	188	695 [12]	271
64	195 [4]	+5 [8]	200	706 [12]	283
65	200 [3]	+6 [8]	206	717 [12]	287
66	205 [5]	+5 [9]	210	728 [12]	288
67	215 [6]	+4 [9]	219	739 [12]	296
68	210 [7]	+4 [10]	214	750 [12]	285

Table 4 (contd.)

Notes and sources:

1. Ten Great Years, p. 119. The original figures were in million
   catties, which were converted into metric tons at the rate of one
   ton equals 2,000 catties.

2. Official figures were 250 million tons for 1958 and 275 million
   tons for 1959. These figures are estimated by the author.

3. Edwin F. Jones, "The Emerging Pattern of China's Economic
   Revolution," in An Economic Profile of Mainland China, Joint
   Economic Committee of Congress, Vol. I, Table II, p. 93.

4. Estimated by the author.

5. Although severe natural calamities beset many sectors of the
   country, grain and cotton production in 1966 was officially reported
   as the highest in China's history (NCNA, Dec. 27, 1966).

6. According to Anna Louise Strong, output for 1967 was 230 million
   tons (Letters from China, No. 55, January 15, 1968). This figure
   is considered inflated. A 10-million-ton increase is assumed by
   the author.

7. Estimated by the author.

8. Dwight H. Perkins, in China in Crisis, edited by Ping-ti Ho and
   Tang Tsou (Chicago: University of Chicago Press, 1968), Vol. I,
   Book 2, p. 663.

9. Carl Riskin, in The Cultural Revolution: 1967 in Review (Michigan
   Papers in Chinese Studies, 1968, No. 2), p. 52.

10. Commonwealth Secretariat, Grain Bulletin, March 1969.

Notes and Sources for Table 4 (contd.)

11. T'ung-chi Kung-tso (Statistical Work), Peking, No. 11, June, 1957, p. 25. These figures are mid-year population.

12. Estimated by the author at an annual growth rate of 1.5%. This rate is based on official figures between 1958-1964; see Robert Michael Field, "A Note on the Population of Communist China," The China Quarterly, No. 38 (April-June, 1969), p. 162.

The foregoing brief summary of the three major economic indicators brings out two basic trends in the Chinese economy.

First, as we noted earlier, the economy progressed in wave-shaped movements, with 1952, 1956, 1958, and 1966 as peaks and 1955, 1957, 1961, and 1967 as troughs. Generally, there was a one-year lag between the growth rate of agriculture and changes in national income and industrial output. [34] The growth rate of national income reached its first peak point, 22.3 percent, in 1952 and then moved downward through 1953 to the lower point of 5.7 percent in 1954. It moved upwards again to its second peak of 14 percent 1956 and declined drastically to 4.6 percent in 1957. In 1958, the year of the Great Leap, it rose sharply to 34 percent before it declined again. A new cycle started in 1962, with 1966 as the new peak. The upswing was then disrupted by the Cultural Revolution. Such cyclical fluctuations are similar to those in a market-oriented, free-enterprise economy; they are quite in conflict with the commonly held view that under a system of central planning the socialist economy can be free of such periodic fluctuations.

Second, throughout the whole period under review there was a wide disparity between the growth of agriculture and industry. While the average annual growth rate of industrial output between 1952 and 1966 amounted to 11 percent, the growth rate for agriculture (measured by grain output) was 2.1 percent - merely keeping pace with population growth. Despite the rapid growth of the modern sector, agriculture is still the dominant part of the Chinese economy. During 1952-57, the agricultural sector accounted for 43.5 percent of net domestic product and 72.9 percent of the labor force. [35] The stagnation or slow growth in agricultural output set a constraint on the growth of industry. The general slowdown of economic growth in the 1960-68 period was mainly caused by the sluggishness of agricultural production. This fact, which dominated the Chinese economy in the past two decades, probably will continue in the foreseeable future.

(III) The Changes in Economic Structure

The disparity between the growth rates of industry and agriculture brought about a radical change in the structure of the economy.

One salient feature was the gradual enhancement of the share of industry and the concomitant decline of agriculture. In pre-war China, about 64.5 percent of national income came from agriculture. This situation remained comparatively unchanged during the early years of Communist control. After the inception of the First Five-Year Plan, however, industry's share of national income rose strikingly, from 18.1 percent in 1952 to 25.9 percent in 1957; it advanced further, to 31.3 percent in 1959. In contrast, the share of agriculture declined steadily from 47.9 percent in 1952 to only 29.9 percent in 1959 (Table 5).

It is interesting to note that the decline in the share of agriculture occurred at roughly the same speed in China during 1952-57 as in the Soviet Union during 1928-40, about 17 percentage points per decades. However, the expansion of the modern sector (including industry, construction, and transportation) was much more rapid in China: 21 percentage points per decade, as against 14 percentage points for the Soviet Union.[36] This might suggest that the pace of Chinese industrialization in the first decade was faster than in the Soviet Union.

The second significant change in the economic structure was the shift in the relative importance of capital good and consumer goods in total industrial output. According to official statistics, between 1952 and 1958 the gross output value of capital good increased by 5.3 fold, while gross output value of consumer goods rose by only 1.4 fold. By 1958 the output value of capital goods already surpassed that of consumer good (Table 6). While the picture may be somewhat distorted by the policy of overpricing capital goods relative to consumer goods[37], the much higher rate of growth in the capital goods industry can be seen from a comparison of annual growth rates of nine branches of the capital goods industry and four branches of the consumer goods industry during 1949-57[38]:

	1949-57	1952-57
Electricity	20.6	21.6
Coal	19.1	14.6
Petroleum	36.5	27.3
Ferrous metals	53.8	28.7
Nonferrous metals	46.5	29.9
Metal processing	40.3	22.1
Chemicals	43.1	25.7
Building materials	30.0	19.3
Timber	18.5	14.8
Textiles	13.5	6.5
Paper	28.8	17.1
Food	14.1	9.3
Everyday commodities	15.0	11.8

Table 5

Structure of Net Domestic Product, 1952–59

Sector	1952	1955	1957	1959
Agriculture	47.9	44.7	40.0	29.9
Industry	18.1	21.8	25.9	31.3
Construction	2.5	3.5	4.7	6.7
Transport	6.6	6.5	6.4	6.7
Trade	13.5	12.5	11.8	12.7
Government Administration	4.6	4.8	5.2	5.1
Other	6.7	6.2	5.8	7.6
Total	100.0	100.0	100.0	100.0

Source: Alexander Eckstein, Communist China's Economic Growth and Foreign Trade (New York: McGraw-Hill, 1966), p. 47.

Table 6

Shares of Capital and Consumer Goods
in Total Gross Industrial Output, 1949-58

Year	Capital goods	Consumer goods
1949	26.6	73.4
50	29.6	70.4
51	32.2	67.8
52	35.6	64.4
53	37.3	62.7
54	38.5	61.5
55	41.7	58.3
56	45.5	54.5
57	48.4	51.6
58	57.3	42.7

Source: Ten Great Years, p. 90.

The ascendancy of industry over agriculture and the supremacy of capital goods over consumer goods substantially changed the distribution of national income. The result was a high rate of capital formation at the expense of living standards.

During the First Plan period, when statistics are available, the share of accumulation in national income rose consistently, from 19.7 percent in 1952 to 23.7 percent in 1957. Concomitantly, the share of consumption declined, from 90.3 percent in 1952 to 76.3 percent in 1957 (Table 7).

The high rate of accumulation and the concentration of investment in the capital goods industry were crucial factors for the high rate of growth achieved, not only in industry but also in the entire economy during the first decade of industrialization. However, they also created stresses and strains on the consumer goods sector. Consumption in China, even in 1952, was much nearer to the bare subsistence level than that in the USSR in 1928. The USSR was able to reduce the consumption proportion from about 84 percent in 1928 to 60 percent in 1940, and to still lower proportions in the 1950's. But Communist China was unable to reduce the share of consumption to below 70 percent. According to the Liu-Yeh study, per capita consumption in 1952 was only 87.3 percent of 1933 and in 1957 about 96.9 percent of 1933.[39] This would suggest that a status of industrial power was achieved partially at the expense of living standards.

Table 7

Ratios of Accumulation and Consumption
in National Income, 1952-57

Year	Accumulation	Consumption
1952	19.7	90.3
53	22.4	77.6
54	22.7	77.3
55	21.6	78.4
56	24.4	75.6
57	23.7	76.3

Source: Yang Po, "The Relation Between Accumulation and Consumption in the National Income of Our Country," Hsin-hua Pan-Yueh-k'an (New China Semi-Monthly), No. 22, 1958.

(IV) Factors Contributing to Economic Growth

Many factors contributed to the rapid advance of the economy
in the first decade. The increase in capital stock, the rise in employment, and improvement in production technology all played a role.
In addition, the availability of foreign assistance also was indispensable
for economic development.

The most significant factor contributing to the economic
growth of 1952-59 was the great augmentation of capital stock.
In the pre-war period (1931-36), the rate of investment (ratio of
gross domestic capital formation to gross domestic product) in
terms of 1933 prices was only 5 percent and in terms of 1952 prices
7.5 percent. However, during the 1952-57 period, the rate of investment in terms of 1952 prices rose sharply, to 24 percent (Table 8).
Compared with rates in other underdeveloped countries in Asia ,
Communist China's rate of investment was rather high. According
to United Nations statistics, the rate of investment for Burma,
Nationalist China (Taiwan), Thailand, India, Ceylon, and the Philippines
in 1952-57 were respectively 24, 20, 17, 16, 14, 11 and 9 percent.
The Chinese investment rate roughly equaled that in the Soviet Union
for 1937, 1950, and 1955 (about 22 percent, according to Abram
Bergson's estimates).[41]

Based on per capita product, China belongs to the lowest
per capita product group in Professor Kuznets' groupings. Yet,
China's investment proportion was similar to the average of the
highest income groups (21.4 percent for Group I and 23.4 percent
for Group II).[42] This clearly indicated that Communist China's
draft industrialization program in the first 10 years was much more
intensive when compared with other countries in the world.

The pattern of Chinese capital investment was unique.
During 1952-57, of the total state investment in terms of current
prices, 51.3 percent went to industry, 8.1 percent to agriculture,
and 16.5 percent to transportation and communications. Compared
with other Asian countries, China invested a much higher share in
industry and a much lower share in agriculture. As a result,
production capacity in industry expanded considerably. Between
1953-59, some 1,795 large industrial projects were wholly or partly
completed. By 1958, 50 percent of the industrial output came from
the newly constructed capacity.[43]

Table 8

Rates of Capital Investment, 1931-36 and 1952-59
(in 1952 prices)

Year	Gross domestic capital formation (in billion yuan)	Gross domestic product (in billion yuan)	Rate of Investment (%)
1931	4.10	62.34	6.6
32	4.44	64.11	6.9
33	4.66	63.91	7.3
34	4.19	59.53	7.0
35	5.16	63.55	8.1
36	6.07	67.56	9.0
1952	14.56	74.67	19.5
53	18.81	78.99	23.8
54	20.31	83.31	24.4
55	21.46	86.57	24.5
56	26.04	97.28	26.8
57	23.72	100.82	23.5
58	26.94	117.71	22.9
59	32.00	127.98	25.0
Average 1931-36	4.77	63.50	7.5
1952-57	20.82	86.94	24.0

Table 8 (contd.)

Source: K. C. Yeh "Capital Formation," in Economic Trends in
Communist China, op. cit., p. 511.

Between 1952 and 1959, a period for which statistics are more complete, a high rate of government capital investment correlated positively with a high rate of industrial output and national income, as exhibited in the cases of 1952, 1956, and 1958. On the other hand, a moderate rate of investment always led to small increases in industrial output and national income, as witnessed in 1955 and 1957 (Table 9). The relationship between the rates of growth of capital construction and of industry is very strong (r=0.94). It is therefore plausible to conclude that the most significant factor contributing to economic growth in the first decade of Communist China was the high rate of capital formation.

The contribution of the labor force to the economic growth has been a controversial subject to study, due to the divergent estimates of nonagricultural employment. For the year 1952, three independent estimates by Hollister, Emerson, and Liu-Yeh give 21.02 million, 36.75 million, and 59.39 million respectively.[44] These differences, arising from divergence in coverage, prevent any meaningful estimate of labor productivity.

In the industrial sector, for which official employment statistics are available and are considered by Western economists as consistent and reliable, the increase in the labor force was significantly lower than the rise in output. This means a constant rise in labor productivity. Based on official employment data and on an independently calculated value-added to industrial output, Robert M. Field estimates that industrial workers' productivity in the 1952-57 period rose by 40.2 percent with an annual growth rate of 7 percent.[45] The rise in industrial labor productivity, however, was the outcome of the rapid increase of capital stock in this sector. During the 1952-57 period, real capital stock in industry not only increased faster than employment but also, after 1953, increased faster than output. The substantial increase in labor productivity was accompanied by a steadily rising capital-labor ratio and a declining productivity of capital stock.[46] This would imply that without a substantial rise in capital stock, the growth of labor productivity in industry would not have occurred.

Progress in technology also played a part in the rise of labor productivity. This was signified by the increase in technical manpower in the modern sector and the introduction of thousands of innovations in production.

Prior to 1949, China possessed a very meager number of engineers and technicians. In 1952, out of a total labor force of 5 million in the industrial sector, only 164,000, or 3 percent, were engineers and technicians. With the advent of large-scale industrialization in 1953, strenuous efforts were made to expand technical manpower. The total number of engineers and technicians in 1957 rose to 449,000, an increase of 180 percent.[47] This rate of increase in technical manpower was more than double that for all industrial workers (80 percent), which means that the industrial labor force contained an increasing proportion of technical manpower.

The emphasis on human capital was also demonstrated by the sharp rise in government outlays for education and scientific research. State expenditures for education at all levels, which amounted to only 813 million yuan in 1951, rose to 2,906 million yuan in 1957 -- a three-fold increase in six years -- and by 1960 had leaped to 6,400 million yuan, or more than double the amount in 1957. Remarkable increases were also registered in state expenditures for scientific research: they leaped from only 11 million yuan in 1952 to 293 million yuan in 1957 and 1,081 million yuan in 1960, an increase of almost 100 times in eight years.[48]

The growth of technical manpower and the acceleration of research and development bore far-reaching consequences for industrial growth, as evidenced by the steady increase of new products, the wide adoption of new innovations, and the constant changes in product mix.[49]

Rapid increases in both physical and human capital, however, would not have been achieved without assistance from the Soviet Union. On the eve of the First Five-Year Plan, China faced an embargo from the West for her participation in the Korean War. Soviet supplies met China's urgent need for equipment and materials. Official Soviet statistics show that between 1950 and 1962, the USSR supplied China with a total of 3 billion dollars' worth of equipment and machinery. Of this total, about 1.8 billion dollars was for the delivery of complete equipment for plants.[50] Without this supply of capital goods, the pace of Chinese industrialization would have slowed down greatly.

Table 9

Annual Percentage Changes in Government Investment,
Industrial Employment, National Income, and
Gross Industrial Output, 1949-59

Years	Government investment[1]	Industrial Employment[2]	National income[3]	Gross industrial output[1]
1949-50	n. a.	27. 9	18. 6	36. 3
1950-51	108. 0	25. 2	17. 0	37. 8
1951-52	85. 5	23. 3	22. 3	30. 2
1952-53	83. 4	15. 5	14. 0	30. 2
1953-54	13. 3	3. 0	5. 7	16. 2
1954-55	2. 5	1. 4	6. 5	5. 6
1955-56	60. 0	27. 0	14. 0	28. 2
1956-57	-6. 7	1. 1	4. 7	11. 4
1957-58	93. 0	84. 9	34. 0	67. 9
1958-59	18. 7	n. a.	22. 0	40. 0

Sources:

1. Alexander Eckstein, "Economic Fluctuation in Communist China," op. cit., p. 716.

2. Ten Great Years, p. 131.

3. Ibid., p. 20.

In the 1949-59 period, the backbone of China's industrialization program was laid by the construction of 156 major Soviet-aided industrial projects. The entire industrial investment plan was built around them. They form the hard core of Chinese modern industry, the parent plants for their special fields and the models for future development. Total investment for the 156 projects and their subsidiaries amounted to 51.5 percent of the total capital investment in industry under the First Five-Year Plan.[51] Consequently, the relative share of these enterprises in the increase in industrial productive capacity was extremely high (Table 10).

At the inception of industrialization, China found her supply of technical and scientific manpower far from adequate. To train a new technical force would have required ten or twenty years. The Soviet decision to dispatch more than 10,000 technicians and specialists to China in different periods filled much of the gap.[52] Had China been deprived of this timely aid, her plans for rehabilitation and reconstruction would have suffered.

The factors which had fostered the rapid growth in the first decade changed dramatically after 1960. A setback in economic growth in 1961-64 was caused by the sharp drop in agricultural production, the sudden suspension of Soviet aid, and the drastic cutback of capital investment.

Until 1958, agricultural production, though lagging behind industrial output, had been rising continuously. In the next three years, food grain output dropped by 20 percent, and China began to import food on a hugh scale. From December 1960, when the first shipments arrived, to the end of 1966, about 24.5 million metric tons of grain were imported from abroad. The agricultural crisis of 1959-61 seriously reduced the country's capacity to invest. It adversely affected the supply of raw materials. This, in turn, hampered industrial output. According to T. C. Liu, an increase of one yuan in agricultural output tends to raise the industrial output by 0.81 yuan.[54] David Denny, using the 1956 figures, has calculated that a 10 percent decline in agricultural production would lead to a decline in industrial output in the following year of 7.8 percent.[55] The sharp decline in agricultural output was the most prominent factor retarding the Chinese economy during the 1960's.

Table 10

Percentage Share of the 156 Soviet-Aided Projects
in the Total Increase in Industrial Capacity
Under the First Five-Year Plan

Industry	Unit	Increase in pro-ductive capacity, 1952-57	Share of 156 Soviet-aided projects (%)
Iron	1,000 tons	5,750	92.1
Steel	"	6,100	82.8
Steel products	"	4,440	90.4
Coal	"	93,100	22.7
Trucks	1,000 units	90	100.0
Power-generating equipment	1,000 tons	800	45.0
Nitrogenous fertilizer	1,000 tons	910	28.5
Crude oil	1,000 tons	3,500	51.4
Metallurgical equipment	1,000 tons	190	50.3

Source: Chu-yuan Cheng, Economic Relations Between Peking and Moscow, 1949-63 (New York: Praeger, 1964), p. 43.

At the same time that agriculture was declining, the Soviet government, in the summer of 1960, suddenly suspended all economic assistance to China. This created a great strain on the already weakened economy. The wholesale withdrawal of Soviet technicians and the halt in Soviet supplies of machinery and equipment caused serious disruptions in the construction of Soviet-aided industrial projects.

Confronting these difficulties, Peking was forced to revise its program for economic development. Government investment dropped considerably in 1961 and 1962. Net domestic investment in 1962 was estimated at a magnitude similar to that in 1953.[56] Large-scale basic construction resumed only after 1965. Despite a 20 percent increase in capital investment in 1966, the absolute level of investment probably was still below that of 1958-59. New policies to conserve manpower in construction and industry were essential because of the food shortage in the urban areas and the need for additional manpower in agriculture. During 1960-61, 20 million worker and urban residents were sent back to the countryside.

The slow recovery which started in 1963 probably was made possible by two factors: the fuller utilization of existing capacity built in 1953-60, and the continuous progress in technology. In November 1962, Yang Ying-chieh, vice-chairman of the State Planning Commission, made it clear that given the present overall economic policy, the direction for the development of heavy industry should be "to make full use of the existing productive capacity, improve product quality, increase product variety, and co-ordinate production of parts and equipment so that we will establish new industries not now in existence in the country."[57] As a consequence of these new endeavors, both labor and capital productivity began to rise steadily leading to the recovery of the modern sector from its trough of 1961.

(V) Non-Economic Elements Affecting Growth

There were many non-economic factors that also significantly affected China's economic development. Three of the most important were ideology, organization, and the centralized planning system.

Confronted with persistent bottlenecks in agriculture and in capital formation, the Chinese leaders have since the very beginning of the new government attempted to substitute ideological inputs and organizational changes for scarce capital resources. Mao Tse-tung has long held that man is potentially most valuable if he is properly indoctrinated and committed. Following this vision of "Communist man," the Chinese Party leader has viewed ideological indoctrination, mass mobilization, and organization as possible substitutes for expertness, professionalism, and the availability of capital equipment.[58]

The primacy of ideology produced positive effects in the early period of institutional transformation and economic rehabilitation. Without the ideological commitment, the fierce class struggle which underlay the land reform, 3-anti and 5-anti[59] campaigns of 1949-52 would have been difficult to carry out so effectively. Obsession with ideology, however, tends to downgrade economic rationale in policy-making and to de-emphasize material incentives as a driving force for production.

During the past two decades, the pendulum has swung -- from an emphasis on material incentives from 1953 to 1957, to a stress on non-material incentives in 1958-60, then a return to material incentives in 1961-65, and back again to non-material incentives in 1966-68. The flows and ebbs always coincided with the changing attitude toward ideological primacy. In those periods when the policy gave priority to ideology, the regime adopted many irrational systems which raised barriers to increasing production. Since the accent was on a egalitarian spirit and self-sacrifice, wages were not used as a proper stimulant to improvement of skills and increased productivity. In rural areas, this egalitarian tendency took the form of foodgrain distribution on grounds mainly unrelated to either work input or output.[60] These irrational measures always caused a drop or stagnation in production.

In the wake of the tragic failure of the Great Leap and communization, the leadership was forced to shift its policy to place primary emphasis on material incentives. Among those measures were the renewed emphasis on piece-rate wages for workers, the return of small plots of land to peasants, and the shift from normative appeals to remunerative appeals. These concessions led to a recovery in agriculture and industry. However, since ideological dogma is so deeply seated in the top leader's mind, once production was on the upswing, the policy was shifted again in favor of non-material incentives and ideological zeal. The new drive finally developed into the Cultural Revolution, which inflicted numerous disruptive effects on the economy. The adherence to ideological dogma and the adoption of many measures which were not congruent with the peasantry's own scale of preferences have been important disruptive forces in Chinese economic progress during the past two decades.

The centralized planning system in industry and agriculture also brought mixed blessings to the economy. The chief merit of a planning system lies in its ability to concentrate scarce resources to achieve the planners' main goals. However, the Chinese planning system was still extremely primitive in its concepts, methods, and practices. It inherited many defects from the Soviet system and at the same time added more of its own.

As is already well-known, any system of planning involves a succession of activities which follow the statement of general goals submitted to the planners by the top decision-makers. [61] Due to the underdeveloped nature of the Chinese economy, there were many handicaps in drawing and implementing a centralized plan.

First, an effective plan relies on adequate and accurate information. The Chinese statistical system was generally rather poor before the Communists took over and made only slow improvement after 1952. Certain types of information were neither collected nor solicited. The planning authorities were left in the dark about such basic information as the size of population and crop acreage. There was little reliable data from the agricultural and handicraft sectors. Weaknesses in the statistical system greatly impeded attempts to plan the economy.

Second, Chinese industrial output was produced by a large number of enterprises that varied widely in scale and used techniques ranging from the very primitive to the most modern. In 1952, there were some 170,000 individual industrial establishments, 80 percent of which were small-scale, each employing less than fifteen persons. [62] Cost disparities among different plants were so wide that a centralized plan to co-ordinate all industrial inputs and outputs became practically infeasible.

Third, the Chinese economy was predominately dependent on agriculture, which is sensitive to weather conditions. The high fluctuations in harvests made a long-term plan extremely difficult.

Since the statistical basis for a large part of the economy was too shaky to support either the sound formulation or the checking of plans, the planning system had many deficiencies. Despite the government's desperate efforts to create a set of guidelines for the nation's industrialization, the planners failed to formulate a long-range program based on sound economic reasoning. The development plans of the past twenty years were developed by trial and error instead of being guided by a well-conceived policy. Policy frequently shifted from one pole to another, depending on the prevailing political atmosphere and the leadership's improvisations. As we noted previously, the pattern of growth was characterized by continuous fluctuations.

There were also many drawbacks in implementing plans. In industry, the persistent tendency of factory managers has been to emphasize attainment of quantity and value of output goals while paying less attention to targets of quality, variety, and costs. The firms tended to be interested only in their own production rather than in the actual needs of those who purchased and used their products. As a result, the entire supply system was very unreliable. A deficit in supply of inputs at some producing units led to underfulfillment of output targets, with potentially serious secondary effects throughout the economy. In agriculture, the ineffectiveness of planning was attributable not only to the rigid use of industrial planning methods but also to central interference with the minutiae of local decisions and to lack of accurate information about the complexity of local conditions. The list of monumental blunders is very long. [63]

The frequent shake-ups in agricultural and industrial organization also caused disruptions in production. Before 1957, China
adopted a highly centralized system wherein all major industries
were directly controlled by the corresponding ministries in Peking.
During 1958 there began a decentralization program. Many industrial
enterprises were to be subject to greater local influence. A "central-
local dual leadership system" was to be followed. By June 1958,
some 80 percent of the enterprises and institutions controlled in
1957 by the industrial ministries of the central government had
been handed over to provinces. Profits of the decentralized enterprises were divided, with 20 percent going to local authorities and
80 percent to the central government. Meanwhile, the number of
mandatory targets was also reduced, from twelve to only four
(total quantitative output of major products, total number of employees,
total wage bill, and profits). However, since 1964, the trend has
gradually swung back: local light industrial enterprises and agricultural
machinery enterprises were again put under central ministries'
control. [64]

In the agricultural sector, barely was land reform complete,
in 1952, when peasant households were organized first into mutual-
aid teams and then into elementary cooperatives. At the beginning
of 1957, the nation's farmers were incorporated into 750,000 collective
farms. One year later, they were again reorganized, into 26,000
people's communes. During subsequent years, the commune system
underwent a series of drastic changes. [65] By 1964, the size of communes
was reduced to only one-third of the original, and the number of
communes was expanded to 74,000.

The frequent shifts in organization of production created
a state of uncertainty among the local administrators, as well as
among workers and peasants.

While the emphasis on ideological and institutional inputs
has its special merits in the economic development of an underdeveloped country, too much of it becomes an increasingly irritating
and retarding factor in economic growth. In the early period, when
material incentives and professionalism gained ground, the economy
registered rapid progress. After 1958, as the policy gradually
shifted to non-material incentives and in favor of party control over
professionals, the economy began to decline. Recovery after the
autumn of 1962 coincided with the return to material incentives to
peasants and workers and in favor of the professionals at the expense

of party control. The Cultural Revolution signaled a revival of a non-material incentive policy. Although its consequences are not yet completely clear, some disruptive effect is already discernible.

(VI) Recent Developments and Prospects

According to the original schedule, the Third Five-Year
Plan was to start in 1963, but this was delayed by the economic
crisis which developed in the aftermath of the Great Leap. The plan
was officially launched in 1966. Toward the end of 1965, on the eve
of the new plan, debates about the future course of economic development became increasingly intense. Those who were in power within
the Party apparently favored continued relaxation of control over
agriculture and decentralization in industrial management as a stimulus to production. At the same time, they also opposed any attempt
at a new Great Leap, lest it produce acute dislocation again. These
views were antithetical to Mao's concept, and the conflict between
the two became one of the factors which culminated in the outbreak
of the Cultural Revolution.

For more than three years, China's political and social
organization suffered an unprecedented upheaval. In the first year
of struggle, the rival Party leaders did not seem to have ruled
out the possibility of a reconciliation, and they had agreed to keep
the economy intact. The 16-point resolution adopted by the Party's
eleventh plenary session in August 1966 provided protection for
scientists, technicians, and workers. Until November 1966, Red
Guards were prohibited from interfering with production in factories,
mines, and communes. Under such precautions the economy showed
no sign of serious damage. [66]

The turning point came in December 1966, when the Party
leaders failed to reach a reconciliation and the Red Guards' attacks
were extended to managers in factories. Since the beginning of 1967,
struggles for power have broken out in almost every factory. The
Maoist leaders mobilized revolutionaries to seize power from the
established officials. This was followed by bitter conflicts among
the factional revolutionary rebels themselves. From May to September
1967, the country's industrial centers were nearly paralyzed.
Throughout the whole year, there were very few official claims about
industrial progress. The usual quarterly or semi-annual announce-
ments of increased production were largely absent. In his address
before a mass meeting in Wuhan on October 9, 1967, Chou En-
lai openly admitted that a "certain price" for the Cultural Revolution
had been paid. "Production is affected to some extent, especially
in places where disturbances occur." [67]

The degree of setback can be roughly measured by the subsequent increase in industrial output in the second half of 1968,
as compared with the first half of 1968 or the corresponding period
of 1967. In those provinces and cities where the Maoist group had
grasped a firmer hold and the Revolutionary Committee had been
set up at an earlier date, industrial output resumed its upward
growth in the second quarter of 1968. For instance, in Heilungkiang,
gross industrial output value in the second quarter was up 22 percent
compared with that in the first quarter. It rose still another 26.9
percent in the third quarter. [68] Thus, the third quarter output
amounted to 155 percent of the first.

In most cases, a sharp rise in industrial output did not emerge
until the second half of 1968. The July output in Shensi was reported
to have achieved a 100 percent increase over the average monthly
output for the first half of 1968. [69] In Kwangsi, total value of industrial
output in its four major industrial centers (Nanning, Liuchow,
Kueilin, and Wuchow) in the fourth quarter equalled or exceeded the
sum of the previous three quarters. [70]

The growing body of evidence illustrates a clear trend;
industrial output in China went up sharply in the second half of
1968. The magnitude of the increase ranged from 50 to 100 percent
compared with the first half. If the Cultural Revolution had left
industry intact, the proclaimed increases in the second half of
1968 would imply a fantastic great leap, which conflicts with the
diminuation of capital investment and the deterioration of the production environment. The staggering rise of output can therefore
only be explained by the depth to which production had previously
sunk.

This assumption gains further support when official reports
contrasting 1968 and 1969 output with that of 1966 are examined.
According to one report, industrial output of Tientsin in August 1968
surpassed that in August 1966 by only 7.4 percent. [71] For most
major industrial centers, it was not until the first quarter or first
half of 1969 that industrial output value exceeded the 1966 level.
In Shanghai, it surpassed 1966 levels by 18 percent, while in Canton
the margin was only 10 percent. [72] The narrow margin between
1969 and 1966 output would suggest that, while the 1968 industrial
output might be only slightly below the 1966 level, the 1967 industrial
output must have declined by 15-20 percent from that of the previous
year. If the 1969 industrial output is 15 percent higher than 1966

and the 1970 output gains another 10 percent increase over 1969,
the increase in industrial output in the Third Five-Year Plan will
be about 45 percent (with 1965 as base), an annual growth rate of
7.7 percent. This is significantly lower than the growth rate between
1957 and 1966 (9.5 percent per year).

The growth of agricultural production does not seem to have
been seriously disturbed in 1966 and 1967, thanks to exceptionally
favorable weather. The 1968 output however, was apparently adversely
affected. By 1970 grain output is expected to be around 225 million
tons, up 12.5 percent from 1965 with an average annual growth rate
of 2.4 percent. Although the growth rate of foodgrains still slightly
exceeded that of population (estimated at 1.5 percent per year),
the margin is narrow indeed.

From a 1969 vantage point it seems that the long-term
prospects of the Chinese economy will be clouded by several unsur-
mounted difficulties.

First of all, there is an apparent barrier to the economy's
attaining a high rate of capital formation. As long as agricultural
output grows at only a snail's pace and the government has to commit
a significant portion of foreign exchange to importing foodgrains, the
rate of capital formation cannot be expected to be high. The recent
emphasis on labor-intensive, small-scale plants and the dispatch
of millions of workers and students to rural areas signifies the
leadership's awareness of the critical shortage of capital. Since
capital remains the most significant factor in economic growth,
a low rate of capital formation will undoubtedly induce a slackening
of the growth rate.

Secondly, in the allocation of scarce resources there is
a growing competition between military and civilian production.
During the 1958-68 period, despite a marked slowdown in the growth
rate, the government spent an increasing proportion of investment
for its nuclear program. Between 1964 and 1969, ten nuclear weapons
tests were conducted. Of the eight ministries of machine-building
industry, six now specialize in defense production. The expansion
of the nuclear weapons program has absorbed a substantial number

of the best scientists, engineers, and managers from the civilian sector. In an economy where such skills are scarcer than in advanced economies, and where they are most critical for the successful and smooth operation of an industrial enterprise because of the workers' generally lower level of knowledge and experience, negative effects are likely to follow when such skills are diverted to other needs. According to a study by Robert Dernberger, during the 1953-65 period a one-yuan increase in domestic production of military goods would cause a reduction in total civilian output of 2.37 yuan.[73] An expansion in defense production will scale down the future growth rate.

Finally, with the advent of the Cultural Revolution, there is a strong tendency for the leadership to substitute ideological inputs for capital and to resume non-material incentives for workers and peasants. Many radical measures similar to those tried during the Great Leap have been resurrected in recent years including the reinstallation of the mass line, the downgrading of engineers and technicians, and tighter control over the rural economy. The anti-material incentive, anti-modern technology mentality, if allowed full sway, will hinder the growth of the economy in general and of the modern sector in particular.

The combined effect of these factors means a lower rate of growth for the Chinese economy in the years ahead. In the coming decade, taking all factors into consideration, an annual growth rate of 2 to 3 percent for the net national product, 6 to 7 percent for industrial output, and 2 to 2.5 percent for agricultural output would be the most likely possibilities for Chinese economic performance.

(VII) Concluding Remarks

Economic developments in Communist China during the
past two decades have driven home some conclusions which might be
useful to other underdeveloped countries.

First of all, despite the extreme backwardness of the inherited economy, with a substantial rise in capital investment and the
importation of foreign technology Communist China has quite success-
fully launched a drafted industrialization program. During the 1953-
59 period, progress in heavy industrial production was very impressive,
and transportation facilities also were expanded. In terms of gross
output value, the annual industrial growth rate was about 11 percent
for the period between 1952-66, a rate comparable to that in the
Soviet Union during 1928-58, which was estimated at 11.7 percent. [74]
A complete heavy industrial complex has been well established,
one which is now capable of producing virtually major machinery
and equipment needed by industry and national defense.

The rapid growth of modern industry has brought about a
gradual change in economic structure. By 1957, the modern sector
was almost equal to the agricultural sector in the share of net domestic
product. Significant change has also been achieved in the pattern of
manufacturing output. According to Hoffman, in the first stage of
industrialization net output of consumer goods industries is on the
average five times that of capital goods. In the second stage the
ratio is reduced to about 2.5 to 1, while in the third stage the net
output of these two groups is approximately equal. Progress from
the first to the third stage takes several decades in most industrial
countries. [75] China, however, reached the third stage in only one
decade; by 1959, net output values of these two groups were almost
equal. This tends to validate Hirschman's and Gerschenkron's
hypothesis that underdeveloped countries today can develop heavy
industry in the initial stages of industrialization, a process that
completely reverses the traditional path of most developed countries,
which started industrialization with consumer goods industries.

The Chinese experiences, however, also illustrate constraints
on the growth of the industrial sector. The rapid growth in the first
decade was achieved through the high rate of capital formation.

As in most underdeveloped economies, agriculture still remains the main source of saving. Despite the rapid growth of the modern sector, at the end of the First Five-Year Plan in 1957, agriculture still dominated the Chinese national product. About 80 percent of raw materials for the consumer goods industry were derived from agriculture. Approximately half the total fiscal revenue came directly or indirectly from agriculture. Farm produce in raw or processed form accounted for more than 70 percent of exports. [76] These figures serve to indicate the vital significance of agriculture and its contributions to capital formation. [77] The stagnation or slow growth of agriculture set a limit to the growth of light industry, exports, and fiscal revenue, which in turn affected the rate of savings. Chinese Communist policy in the first decade, by concentrating available resources in industrial development, created an increasingly wide gap between agriculture and industry. The sluggishness of agricultural production became a stumbling block for the further advance of industrialization. The Chinese experiences therefore illustrate that in a predominately agrarian economy, the build-up and expansion of heavy industry for the sake of further expansion of heavy industry may bring about impressive economic growth in a short period, but such growth is not sustainable and is bound to slow down.

Finally, the Chinese efforts to use ideological inputs as a substitute for capital achieved only marginal results. The organizational changes in agriculture and the periodic indoctrinations of the rural population did not bring about significant improvement in agricultural output. Instead, material rewards and increases in capital inputs proved to be the key stimulus to production. The Soviet reforms under Khrushchev's rule and the Chinese relaxation during 1961-65 prove that only material incentives and appreciable increases in capital investment can break the agricultural bottleneck and pave the way for sustained growth in industry.

48

Notes

(1) K. C. Yeh, "Soviet and Communist Chinese Industrialization Strategies," in Donald W. Treadgold (ed.), Soviet and Chinese Communism, Similarities and Differences (Seattle: Washington University Press, 1967), pp. 327-363.

(2) Ibid., p. 336.

(3) Ten Great Years (Peking State Statistical Bureau, 1959), pp. 20, 88.

(4) See editorials in Chi-hua Ching-chi (Planned Economy), Peking, No. 9, 1957, pp. 1-4, and No. 10, 1957, pp. 1-3; also articles by Liao Chi-li, Ibid., No. 8, 1957, pp. 4-6; and Chi Chung-wei, Ibid., No. 10, 1957, pp. 7-11.

(5) Liu Shao-ch'i, Report on the Work of the Central Committee of the CCP to the Second Session of the Eight National Congress (Peking: Foreign Language Press, 1958), p. 49.

(6) Ragnar Nurkse, Problems of Capital Formation in Under-developed Areas (Oxford: Blackwell, 1953), p. 49.

(7) Jen-min Jih-pao (People's Daily), May 3, 1958.

(8) For details see Chu-yuan Cheng, Communist China's Economy, 1949-1962 (South Orange, N. J.: Seton Hall University Press, 1963), p. 139.

(9) The stress of the urgency of liberating housewives from domestic chores for socialist construction was enunciated by Finance Minister Li Hsien-nien, in Ts'ai-cheng (Public Finance), No. 8, August 5, 1958.

(10) In 1958, one-third of steel and coal output was produced by small workshops and coal pits.

(11) According to Viscount Montgomery, who visited China in September 1961, Mao personally told him that output of food-grains in 1960 was 150 million tons and the forecast for 1961 was for 10 million tons more (The Sunday Times, London, October 15, 1961, p. 25). If this is true, 1960 output dropped by 20% from 1959 and 30% from 1958.

(12) This new policy was decided at the Ninth Plenum of the Eight
     CCP Central Committee in January 1961 (Jen-min Jih-pao,
     Jan. 21, 1961). The general policy known as "readjustment,
     consolidation, reinforcement, and improvement" was mentioned
     in Kung Hsian-Cheng, "Produce More and Better Light Industrial
     Products for Daily Use, " Hung-ch'i (Red Flag), No. 5, pp. 89-90,
     February 10, 1962.

(13) This change in prioities was officially announced by Chou En-lai
     in his speech of March 27, 1962, to the third session of the
     National People's Congress (JMJP, April 16, 1962).

(14) See article by Ma Wen-Sui (Minister of Labor) in Hung-ch'i,
     No. 5, 1961, p. 11.

(15) For details, see Chu-yuan Cheng, "The Changing Pattern of
     Rural Communes in Communist China, " Asian Survey, Nov. 1961,
     pp. 3-9.

(16) In his December Report to the Third NPC, Chou En-lai pointed
     out that the 1964 agricultural production would surpass that
     of 1957 (JMJP, Dec. 31, 1964).

(17) Chu-yuan Cheng, "The Root of China's Cultural Revolution -
     the fued between Mao Tse-tung and Liu Shao-ch'i, " Orbis,
     Vol. II., No. 4 (1968), pp. 1160-1178.

(18) An excellent analysis is provided by Alexander Eckstein in
     his paper "Economic Fluctuations in Communist China's
     Domestic Development, " in Ping-ti Ho and Tang Tsou (ed.),
     China in Crisis (Chicago: University of Chicago Press, 1968),
     Vol I, Book 2, pp. 669-700.

(19) For instance, chemical fertilizer output in Kiangsu by small
     plants in 1969 was officially reported to be triple that in 1966.

(20) For 1958 figures, see Ten Great Years, p. 20; for 1959 figure,
     see Ching-chi Yen-chiu (Economic Research), No. 6, 1960, p. 15.

(21) T. C. Liu and K. C. Yeh, The Economy of the Chinese Mainland: National Income and Economic Development, 1933-59 (Princeton, N. J. Princeton University Press, 1965), pp. 39-64.

(22) The major contributions are Liu and Yeh, op. cit.; Alexander Eckstein, The National Income of Communist China (Glencoe, Ill.: The Free Press, 1961); and W. W. Hollister, China's Gross National Product and Social Accounts, 1950-57 (Glencoe, Ill.: The Free Press, 1958).

(23) T. C. Liu and K. C. Yeh, op. cit, p. 220.

(24) Ten Great Years, p. 89.

(25) A Chinese official statement admitted that "in computing the constant price of industrial output, there is some overpricing in producers' goods. Comparing the price level of 1952 with that of 1936, it shows an increase of 1.5 times for industrial products in general. Among the industrial products, prices of producers' goods was two-fold that of 1936 while prices for consumers' goods was only one time the amount" (T'ung-chi Kung-tso [Statistical Works], No. 1, Jan. 1957, p. 15).

(26) C. M. Li, Economic Development of Communist China (Berkeley and Los Angeles: University of California Press, 1959), p. 36.

(27) For details see my forthcoming study Machine-Building Industry in Communist China, Chapter 6. Chicago: Aldine Publishing Co.

(28) For comments on Field's indexes, see K. Chao's testimony in Mainland China in the World Economy, (Washington, D. C.: Joint Economic Committee of U. S. Congress, 1967), pp. 134-135: also D. H. Perkins' comment in China in Crisis, op. cit., pp. 664-665.

(29) According to official statistics, 1957, due to shortages of raw materials, the rates of operation in the consumer goods industries were as follow: 85% for textiles, 66% for sugar-making, 75% for oil pressing, 52% for tobacco processing, 68% for flour, 69% for leather and 53% for canned foods" (Hsueh-hsi [Study], No. 20, 1957).

(30) The official target for foodgrain output in 1958 was 375 million tons and for cotton, 3.35 million tons -- all double the figures for 1957.

(31) Chu-yuan Cheng, "Economy and Foreign Trade of Mainland China", in Richard Starr (ed.), Aspects of Modern Communism (Columbia, S. C. University of South Carolina Press, 1968), pp. 242-243.

(32) According to Chou En-lai, supplies of pork, mutton, vegetables, and non-staple foodstuffs in 1964 were 30% higher than in 1957 (JMJP, Dec. 31, 1964).

(33) According to Ta-Kung-pao (Impartial Daily, Peking), Dec. 24, 1963, the output of side-line occupations accounted for 30% of peasants' income in 1963.

(34) Chu-yuan Cheng, Communist China's Economy, 1949-62, op. cit., pp. 160-165; also Alexander Eckstein "Economic Fluctuations in Communist China's Domestic Development," op. cit., pp. 691-729.

(35) T. C. Liu, "Quantitative Trends in the Economy," in Eckstein, Galenson, and Liu (ed.), Economic Trends in Communist China (Chicago: Aldine Press, 1968), p. 127.

(36) Ibid., p. 125.

(37) See note 25.

(38) K. Chao, The Rate and Pattern of Industrial Growth in Communist China (Ann Arbor: University of Michigan Press, 1965), p. 97.

(39) Liu, "Quantitative Trends," op. cit., p. 146.

(40) United Nations, Economic Survey, 1957, pp. 216-217; 1960, p. 129; and 1961, pp. 172-173.

(41) Liu, "Quantitative Trends," p. 128.

(42) Ibid., p. 131. For details of Kuznets' groupings, see his "Quantitative Aspects of Economic Growth of Nations: V" in Economic Development and Cultural Change, July 1960, Table I.

(43) C. M. Li (ed.), Industrial Development in Communist China (New York: Praeger, 1964). p. 19.

(44) Liu, "Quantitative Trends," pp. 109-110.

(45) Robert Michael Field, "Labor Productivity in Industry," in Economic Trends in Communist China, op. cit., p. 658.

(46) According to Field, capital/labor ratio rose by 55.1% between 1952 and 1957, while output per unit of capital (Capital productivity) declined by 9.6% in the same period (Ibid., p. 658).

(47) Chu-yuan Cheng, Scientific and Engineering Manpower in Communist China, 1949-63 (Washington, D. C.: National Science Foundation, 1966), p. 111.

(48) Ibid., pp. 80-81.

(49) For detailed discussions, see Chu-yuan Cheng, Machine-Building Industry in Communist China (forthcoming).

(50) Chu-yuan Cheng, Economic Relations Between Peking and Moscow, 1949-63 (New York: Praeger, 1964), p. 31.

(51) The First Five-Year Plan, p. 79.

(52) Cheng, Scientific and Engineering Manpower, op. cit., pp. 194-5.

(53) These figures are net imports (imports minus exports), quoted from An Economic Profile of Mainland China, op. cit., p. 601.

(54) Liu, "Quantitative Trends," op. cit., p. 161.

(55) David Denny, "Agricultural Marketings in Communist China" (Unpublished ms.), Chapter III.

(56) Liu, "Quantitative Trends," op. cit., p. 164.

(57) Yang Ying-chieh, "On the Problem of Comprehensive Balance in National Economic Planning," Ching-chi Yen-chiu (Economic Research), No. 73, Nov 17, 1962.

(58) Eckstein, "Economic Fluctuations," op. cit., p. 699.

(59) The official purpose of the "3-anti" campaign was to fight the three evils in government officials -- bureaucratism, commandism, and subjectivism. The purpose of the "5-anti" campaign was to combat the evils of capitalists -- bribery of government workers, tax evasion, theft of state property, cheating on government contracts, and stealing economic information. Its real purpose, however, was to curb the increasing growth of the private sector.

(60) Charles Hoffmann, "Work Incentive Policy in Communist China," in C. M. Li (ed.), Industrial Development in Communist China, op. cit., pp. 92-109.

(61) Arcadius Kahan, "Agriculture," in Allen Kassof (ed.), Prospects for Soviet Society (New York: Praeger, 1968), pp. 265-6.

(62) D. H. Perkins, "Industrial Planning and Management," in Economic Trends in Communist China, op. cit.; pp. 604-5.

(63) For some examples of technical mistakes, see Kenneth R. Walker "Organization of Agricultural Production", in Economic Trends in Communist China, op. cit., pp. 420-422.

(64) T'ung Wan: "The Problem of Fixed Point Supply of Third Category Raw Materials for Enterprises in Light Industry," Ching-chi Yen-chiu, No. 2, Feb. 1966, p. 42.

(65) Cheng, Communist China's Economy, 1949-62, op. cit., pp. 48-50.

(66) Chu-yuan Cheng, "The Cultural Revolution and China's Economy," Current History, Sept. 1967, pp. 148-177.

(67) NCNA, Oct. 9, 1967.

(68) JMJP, Aug. 20, 1968, p. 4.

(69) JMJP, Sept. 27, 1968, p. 4.

(70) Kwangsi Jih-pao (Kwangsi Daily), Nanning, Mar. 29, 1969, editorial.

(71) NCNA, Dec. 21, 1968.

(72) Wen Hui Pao, Shanghai, Apr. 10, 1969.

(73) Robert Dernberger, "Opportunity Costs of Defense Expenditures" (unpublished ms).

(74) Herbert S. Levine, "Industry," in Prospects for Soviet Society, op. cit., p. 292.

(75) W. G. Hoffman, The Growth of Industrial Economies (Manchester: Manchester University Press, 1958).

(76) Chi-hua Ching-chi (Planned Economy), Peking, No. 8, 1957, p. 4.

(77) Empirical information supports this view. In the First Plan, growth rates of agricultural production (average of the two previous years) are very closely related to the growth rates of capital construction (r=0.92).

A Bibliography of Selected Materials on
Chinese Economic Development

This bibliography, including materials concerning both the
historical and contemporary economic development of mainland
China, originally was a report submitted to the Summer Seminar on
Economic Development sponsored by the Center for Research on
Economic Development at the University of Michigan during June-
July 1970. The purpose of this bibliography is to provide a general
guide for graduate students who are interested in exploring the Chinese
experience in economic development in a comparative framework.
Since this is not designed as a general research guide, materials
have been included on a very selective basis relating to the topics
outlined on the first page. The bibliography contains only materials
available in the English language. For advanced students, the original
language Chinese materials will be particularly valuable. While most
of the very brief annotations are supplied by the author, some entries
are quoted from Professor Charles O. Hucker's bibliography on
China compiled in 1962. * The materials cited were published largely
before 1969, although some new articles published in 1970 have also
been included.

1. General works

    A. Pre-1949 period

    B. Communist China

2. Strategy for Economic Development

3. Resources of Development

    A. Land and Natural Resources

    B. Population and Labor

    C. Capital Formation

    D. Education and Technology

---

* Charles Hucker, China: A Critical Bibliography, Tucson: University
of Arizona Press, 1962.

4. Industrialization

5. Agricultural Development

6. Public Finance, Domestic and Foreign Trade

7. Income and Standard of Living

8. Economic Planning

9. Major Statistical Works

    A. Evaluation of Official Statistics

    B. Major Sources of Official Statistics

10. Major Periodicals on Chinese Economic Development

1. General Works

    A. Pre-1949 Period

    Allen, G. C. and Audrey G. Donnithorne. Western Enterprise
    in Far Eastern Economic Development: China and Japan. London:
    Allen and Unwin. 1954.
        An analysis of the activities of Western merchants, engineers,
    and financiers in China from the Opium War to the 1950's, with
    an evaluation of their influence on China's general economic
    development.

    Balazs, E. "The Birth of Capitalism in China", Journal of the
    Economic and Social History of the Orient. 111 (1960), 192-216.
        An interpretive study of China's socioeconomic tradition
    to explain why industrial capitalism did not develop indigenously.

    Balazs E. "The Issue of Capitalism in China", in Arthur F.
    Wright (ed.) Chinese Civilization and Bureaucracy, New Haven:
    Yale University Press, 1964, pp 39-54.
        A historical study tracing back the birth of capitalism
    in China to Sung dynasty and pointing out the chief impediments
    of its development.

    Cowan, C. D. (ed.) The Economic Development of China and
    Japan, New York: Praeger, 1964.
        A collection of articles on economic development in China
    and Japan.

    Fairbank, John K., Alexander Eckstein and L. S. Yang. "Economic
    Change in Early Modern China: An Analytic Framework", Economic
    Development and Cultural Change, IX (1960-61), 1-26.
        An analysis of traditional patterns of economic organization
    in 19th century China, emphasizing factors that retarded economic
    growth in Western pattern.

Feuerwerker, Albert,"The Chinese Economy ca. 1870-1911",
Michigan Papers in Chinese Studies, No. 5, 1969.
A thorough analysis of the structure and development of
Chinese agriculture in the 19th century and its implications
for the rest of the economy.

Feuerwerker, Albert,"The Chinese Economy, 1912-1949",
Michigan Papers in Chinese Studies, No. 1, 1968
A general survey of the Chinese economy from the end of
the Manchu dynasty to the establishment of the People's Republic.
The Chinese economy during this period is viewed by the author
as a system of relations among the factors of production neither
grew in size nor altered in structure in any significant degree.

Kirby, E. Stuart, Introduction to the Economic History of China.
London: Allen and Unwin, 1954.
A survey of studies on the socio-economic development of
China throughout history, period by period rather than an economic
history in itself.

Jacobs, Norman, The Origin of Modern Capitalism in Eastern
Asia. Hongkong: Hongkong University Press, 1958.
A sociological study of why capitalism has developed in
modern Japan but not in China.

Lieu, D. K. China's Economic Stabilization and Reconstruction.
New Brunswick: Rutgers University Press, 1948.
A general survey of Nationalist China's plans and projects
for economic development after World War II.

Murphey, Rhoads, "The Treaty Ports and China's Modernization:
What Went Wrong?", Michigan Papers in Chinese Studies,
No. 7, 1970
An appraisal of the impact of treaty ports on China's modern-
ization. The author finds the backwash and multiplier effects
of economic growth in the treaty ports were rather limited.

Paaux, Douglas S. "The Kuomintang and Economic Stagnation,
1928-1937", Journal of Asian Studies, XVI (1956-57), 213-220.
An article criticizing the nationalist government's failures
to promote economic development.

Tawney, Richard Henry. Land and Labor in China. New York: Harcourt, Brace, 1932.

A classical evaluation of China's general economic situation in the earliest years under the nationalist government.

Wang Yu-ch'uan. "The Rise of Land Tax and the Fall of Dynasties in Chinese History", Pacific Affairs, IX (1936), 201-220.

A brief but influential essay suggesting an economic interpretation of China's traditional dynastic cycle.

Young, Arthur N. China's Economic and Financial Reconstruction. Shanghai: Commercial Press, 1947.

An account of the economic development under the nationalist government.

B. Communist China

Adler, Solomon. The Chinese Economy. New York: Monthly Review Press, 1957.

A sympathetic survey of China's over-all economic development under communism during the 1950's.

Chen Nai-Ruenn and Walter Galenson. The Chinese Economy Under Communism. Chicago, Aldine, 1969.

A standard textbook for undergraduate students.

Cheng, Chu-yuan. Communist China's Economy, 1949-62, Structural Changes and Crisis. South Orange, New Jersey: Seton Hall University Press, 1963.

A critical review of Chinese economy during the first 12 years of communist rule with emphasis on the impact of institutional changes on national economy.

Clark, Colin. "Economic Growth in Communist China", China Quarterly No. 21 (Jan-March, 1965) 148-167.

A study of economic growth in China since the 1930's with particular attention to the level of growth that the communist government has stimulated since 1949.

Eckstein, A., W. Galenson and T. C. Liu (eds.) Economic
Trends in Communist China, Chicago: Aldine, 1968.
    An authoritative review of major areas of the Chinese economy
between 1949-65.

Hughes, T. J. and D. E. T. Luard. The Economic Development
of Communist China, 1949-1958. London: Oxford University
Press, 1959.
    A general survey of accomplishments and future prospects
in both agriculture and industry.

Gluckstein, Ygael. Mao' China: Economic and Political Survey.
Boston: Beacon Press, 1957.
    An unsympathetic study on the economic development of
communist China, emphasizing state regimentation of all economic
activities.

Rostow, W. W. et al. The Prospects for Communist China,
New York: Wiley, 1954.
    An analysis of the early economic development of communist
China and of its economic potential.

Stanford Research Institute, The Economic Potential of Communist
China. Menlo Park, Calif: 1964.
    A detailed technical survey of China's economy during 1949-62.

Szezepanik, Edward F. (ed.) Symposium on Economic and Social
Problems of the Far East. Hong Kong: University Press, 1962.
    Many useful analyses of Chinese economy during the 1950's
are included.

U. S. Congress, Joint Economic Committee. An Economic Profile
of Mainland China. Washington, D. C.: Government Printing
Office, 1967, 2 volumes.
    The most useful book on Chinese economy, including more
than 20 articles dealing with every major aspect by specialists
both in universities and the U. S. government.

Wu Yuan-li, An Economic Survey of Communist China. New York: Bookman Associates, 1956.
On China's success in rapid industrialization through harsh overregimentation of labor.

2. Strategy for Economic Development

Barnett, A. Doak. Communist Economic Strategy: The Rise of Mainland China. Washington, D. C.: National Planning Association, 1959.
A general survey of Communist China's economic policies.

Clubb, O. Edmund, "Chinese Communist Development Programs in Manchuria", Secretariat Paper No. 3, New York: Institute of Pacific Relations, 1954.
On the reinvigoration of industry and agriculture in Manchuria from 1950 through 1952.

Eckstein, Alexander, "The Strategy of Economic Development in Communist China", American Economic Review, Papers and Proceedings, Vol. LI, No. 2 (May 1961), pp. 508-517.
An analysis of the policies on economic development in Communist China during 1953-62.

Kashin, A. "The Soviet and Chinese Paths to Communism: Are They Essentially Different?", Bulletin of Institute for the Study of USSR, Vol. VIII, No. 5, (May 1961), pp. 40-44.
A short comparison of the development paths of China and the Soviet Union.

Prybyla, Jan S. "Communist China's Strategy of Economic Development", Asian Survey, Oct. 1966, pp. 589-603.
A comprehensive study of Chinese development strategy in the 1960's after the series of setbacks suffered in the late 1950's and early 1960's.

Schurmann, H. F. "China's New Economic Policy--Transition or Beginning". China Quarterly, Jan.-March, 1964, pp. 65-91.
A detailed account of Chinese economic policies during the early 1960's.

Yeh, K. C. "Soviet and Communist Chinese Industrialization Strategies", in Donald W. Treadgold (ed.), Soviet and Chinese Communism, Seattle: University of Washington Press, 1967.
An excellent comparison of the development strategies in China and the USSR.

3. Resources of Development

A. Land and Natural Resources

Cressey, G. B. China's Geographic Foundations, New York: McGraw-Hill, 1934.
A general survey of the land and the Chinese people's use of it.

Cressey, G. B. Land of the 500 Million, New York: McGraw-Hill, 1955.
The most comprehensive geographical survey of China, the people, the topography, the climate and the resources.

Fei, Hsiao-tung and Chang Chih-i, Earthbound China, Chicago: University Press, 1945.
A sociological analysis of the total economic life of three communities in Yunan province, representing rural agriculture, rural industry and rural commerce.

Mallory, Walter H. China: Land of Famine. New York: American Geographical Society, 1926.
An evaluation of the causes and possible cures of recurrent famines in China.

Wang Kung-ping, "Mineral Resources of China, with special reference to nonferrous metal", Geographical Review, 1944.

Wang Kung-ping, "Mineral Wealth and Industrial Power", Mining Engineering, August, 1960, pp. 901-912.
A brief account of the mineral resources in China.

Wu Yuan-li. Economic Development and the Use of Energy
Resources in Communist China, New York: Praeger, 1963.
A comprehensive study on coal, petroleum and electrical
power in Communist China.

B. Population and Labor

Aird, John Shields. The Size, Composition and Growth of the
Population of Mainland China, Washington, D. C.: Bureau of
the Census, U. S. Dept. of Commerce, 1961.
A sophisticated technical study on Chinese population.

Chandrasekhar, S. China's Population. Hong Kong: Hong Kong
University Press, 1959.
A brief report on the techniques and findings of the mainland
registration of 1953 by a leading Indian demographer who has
visited China and consulted with Chinese demographers.

Ch'en Ta. Population in Modern China, Chicago: University of
Chicago Press, 1946.
An authoritative study of the development of modern demographic methods under the nationalist government, with statistics
and descriptions concerning the demographic aspects of limited
groups of Chinese in the 1940's.

Ch'en Ta. New China's Population Census of 1953 and Its
Relations to National Reconstruction and Demographic Research,
Stockholm: International Statistical Institute, 1957.

Emerson, John Philip. Nonagricultural Employment in Mainland
China, 1949-58, Washington, D. C.: Bureau of Census, U. S.
Dept. of Commerce, 1965.
An important monograph on nonagricultural labor in Communist
China.

Ho Ping-ti. Studies on the Population of China, 1368-1953, Cambridge:
Harvard University Press, 1959.
A thorough, authoritative analysis of the techniques and findings
of Chinese census registrations in modern centuries.

64

Hou Chi-ming. "Manpower, Employment, and Unemployment", in Eckstein, Galenson, and Liu (eds.), Economic Trends in Communist China, pp. 329-396.

Orleans, Leo A. "Problems of Manpower Absorbtion in Rural China", China Quarterly, July-Sept. 1961.

C. Capital Formation

Hou, Chi-ming. Foreign Investment and Economic Development in China, 1840-1937, Cambridge: Harvard University Press, 1965.
 A scholarly analysis of the role played by foreign investment in China during the century before 1939.

Hollister, William W. China's Gross National Product and Social Accounts, 1950-57, Glencoe, Ill.: The Free Press, 1958.
 The first study of Communist China's national income and capital formation using the concepts used by the U. S. Department of Commerce.

Ishikawa, Shigeru. National Income and Capital Formation in Mainland China, Tokyo: The Institute of Asian Economic Affairs, 1965.
 A careful examination of official statistics on national income and capital formation by a leading Japanese specialist on the economy of Communist China.

Pauley, Edwin S. A Report on Japanese Assets in Manchuria to the President of the United States, Washington, D. C., 1946.
 An authoritative survey on Japanese investment in Manchuria before 1945 and the destructive effect of the Soviet dismantling of major factories shortly after the Second World War.

Ou Pao-San. Capital Formation and Consumers' Outlay in China, unpublished doctoral dissertation, Harvard University, 1948.

Remer, C. F. Foreign Investment in China, New York: MacMillan, 1933.
A classical study on foreign investment in China during the 1920's and early 1930's.

Yeh, K. C. Capital Formation in Mainland China: 1931-36 and 1952-57, unpublished doctoral dissertation, New York: Columbia University, 1964.

D. Education and Technology

Cheng, Chu-yuan. Scientific and Engineering Manpower in Communist China, 1949-1963, Washington, D. C.: National Science Foundation, 1966.
The first comprehensive analysis of the growth, training and utilization of scientific and technical manpower in China, basing on an intensive study of biographic data of 1, 200 top scientists and engineers now living in mainland China.

Hu, Chang-tu. Chinese Education under Communism, New York: Teacher College, Columbia University, 1962.
A useful book on education in the 1950's.

Orleans, Leo A. Professional Manpower and Education in Communist China, Washington, D. C.: Government Printing Office, 1961.
A detailed analysis of the new educational system in China with regards to the training of technical manpower.

Needham, Joseph. Science and Civilization in China, Cambridge: University Press.
The most authoritative study on the historical development of science and technology in China. The first volume was published in 1954; since then five other volumes have been published.

Sidney, H. (ed.) Science in Communist China, Washington: American Association for the Advancement of Science, 1961.
A collection of papers on various major aspects of scientific and technical development in Communist China during its first decade.

Uchida, Genko. "Technology in China", in Scientific American, Nov. 1966, pp. 37–45.

An objective evaluation of technological level and progress in Communist China by a leading Japanese specialist.

4. Industrialization

Chang, John K. Industrial Development in Pre-Communist China: A Quantitative Analysis, Chicago: Aldin, 1969.

A statistical analysis of industrial growth during the 1930's.

Chao, Kang. The Rate and Pattern of Industrial Growth in Communist China, Ann Arbor: University of Michigan Press, 1965.

An attempt of constructing an index of industrial output during 1952-57.

Chao, Kang. The Construction Industry in Communist China, Chicago: Aldine, 1968.

A study of the growth and input-output relations in Chinese construction industry during the 1950's.

Cheng, Chu-yuan. "The Growth and Structural Changes in Chinese Machine-Building Industry, 1952-1966", China Quarterly, Jan-March, 1970, pp. 26-57.

A systematic analysis of the growth and structural changes in Chinese machinery industry during the first 18 years of Communist control.

Cheng, Yu-kwei. Foreign Trade and Industrial Development of China, Washington, D. C., 1956.

A study of commercial and industrial development from 1910 to 1948, emphasizing developments under the nationalist government in the 1930's.

Feuerwerker, Albert. China's Early Industrialization, Cambridge: Harvard University Press, 1958.

On the nature of the old economic order and 19th century difficulties in transforming it along the lines of Western industrial enterprises, with special reference to the China Merchants' Navigation Company and other officially-sponsored enterprises managed by Shen Huan-huai (1844-1916).

Field, R. Michael, "Industrial Production in Communist China, 1957-1968", The China Quarterly, Apr-June, 1970, pp. 46-64.
  A revised index of industrial production in Communist China during the 1957-68 period.

Li, Choh-ming. Economic Development of Communist China: An appraisal of the First Five Years of Industrialization, Berkeley and Los Angeles: University of California Press, 1959.
  An objective evaluation of the achievements of the First Five-Year Plan.

Li, Choh-ming. (ed.) Industrial Development in Communist China, New York: Praeger, 1964.
  A collection of papers on the various aspects of Chinese industry in the 1950's and early 1960's.

Lieu, D. K. The Growth and Industrialization of Shanghai, Shanghai: Chinese Institute of Economic and Statistical Research, 1936.
  The best single work on the historical account of the growth of Shanghai as well as an analysis on the economic characteristics and social effects of industrialization.

Malenbaum, Wilfred. "India and China: Development and Contrasts", Journal of Political Economy, LXIV (1956), 1-24.
  A comparison of economic development and industrialization during the early years of Communist China with those in the Republic of India.

Ou, Pao-san. "Industrial Production and Employment in Pre-War China", Economic Journal, Vol. 56, Sept. 1946, pp. 426-434.

Schumpter, E. B., et al. The Industrialization of Japan and Manchukuo, New York: MacMillan, 1940.
  Useful accounts on industrial development in Manchuria during the 1930's.

United Nations, Economic Commission for Asian and the Far East. "Industrialization in the Centrally Planned Economy of China", in Economic Survey of Asia and the Far East, 1958.
  An excellent summary and evaluation of industrialization in the First Five-Year Plan of Communist China.

Li, Fu-chun. Report on the First Five-Year Plan for Development of the National Economy of the People's Republic of China in 1953-57, Peking: Foreign Language Press, 1955.
An official account for the First Five-Year Plan.

5. Agricultural Development

Bardhan, Franab, K. "Chinese and Indian Agriculture: A Broad Comparison of Recent Policy and Performance", Journal of Asian Studies, Vol XXIX No. 3, (May, 1970), pp. 515-537.
A comparison of relative performance in agricultural production between India and China during 1952-67 with some discussions on the situation regarding inputs and organization in these two countries.

Chang, C. C. An Estimate of China's Farms and Crops, Nanking: Nanking University, 1933.
Including many major figures on every aspect of Chinese agriculture.

Chang, C. M. "Mao's Strategem of Land Reform", Foreign Affairs, XXIX, July 1951, pp. 550-563.
An analysis of Communist China's land reform policies during the early phase of its control.

Chang, Pei-kang. Agriculture and Industrialization, Cambridge: Harvard University Press, 1941.
An examination of the adjustments that take place as an agricultural country is industrialized, with reference to pre-war China.

Cheng, Chu-yuan. The People's Communes, Hong Kong: Union Research Institute, 1959.
A detailed account of the function and organization structure of China's rural communes during the first phase of existence.

Cheng, Chu-yuan. "The Changing Pattern of Rural Communes in Communist China", Asian Survey, Nov 1961, pp. 3-9.
An analysis tracing the three stages of evolution of China's rural communes during 1958 and 1961.

Chao, Kuo-chun. Agrarian Policy of the Chinese Communist Party, 1952-1959, Bombay: Asia Publishing House, 1960.
An examination of Chinese communist policies on agricultural collectivization.

Buck, John Lossing. Chinese Farm Economy, Nanking: University of Nanking, 1930.
A voluminous statistical study of farm management and various socio-economic aspects of farm life in 2,866 farms of North China, the Yangtze delta region, and the southeast coastal provinces, based on field survey made between 1921 and 1925. A very valuable sourcebook on the state of the agricultural economy in China in the pre-war years.

Buck, John Lossing. Land Utilization in China, 3 vols. Nanking: University of Nanking, 1937. Reprinted ed. of vol 1. New York: Council on Economic and Cultural Affairs, 1956.
The most comprehensive descriptive study ever made on China's modern agricultural economy, based on a survey of 16,786 farms in 22 provinces from 1929 to 1933.

Buck, John Lossing, Owen L. Dawson and Yuan-Li Wu, Food and Agriculture in Communist China, New York: Praeger, 1966.
A collection of three essays on food production and agricultural problems.

Dawson, Owen L. Communists China's Agriculture, Its Development and Future Potential, New York: Praeger, 1970.
A review of recent changes and the current situation of China's farm resources and farm practices.

Jones, P. P. and T. T. Poleman. Communes and the Agricultural Crises in China, Stanford: Stanford Research Institute, 1962.
A short review of the commune system and its impact on Chinese agriculture during the late 1950's.

Mao, Tse-tung. On the Question of Agricultural Cooperativization, Peking: Foreign Languages Press, 1956.
A major speech on the policy line of agricultural collectivization in China.

Kuo, Leslie T. C. "Agricultural Mechanization in Communist China", The China Quarterly, Jan.-March, 1964.
On efforts toward mechanization of agriculture.

Ishikawa, Shigeru. Factors Affecting China's Agriculture in the Coming Decade, Tokyo: The Institute of Asian Economic Affairs, 1967.
  A technical analysis of the input-output relations in Chinese agricultural development.

Liu, Jung-chao. "Fertilizer Applications in Communist China", The China Quarterly, Oct.-Dec. 1965, pp. 28-52.
  Estimates of demand and output in China's chemical fertilizer.

Liu, Jung-chao, "Fertilizer Supply and Grain Production in Communist China", Journal of Farm Economics, Vol. 47, No. 4 (Nov. 1965), pp. 915-932.
  Estimates of the effect of fertilizer supply on grain output.

Perkins, D. H. Agricultural Development in China, 1368-1968, Chicago: Aldine, 1969.
  A major work on the long-term growth of China's agricultural sector.

Provincial Agricultural Statistics for Communist China, compiled by the Committee on the Economy of China, Social Science Research Council and published by the same organization, 1969.
  A collection of agricultural statistical data derived from provincial newspapers published in Chinese mainland during 1949 to 1959.

Schran, Peter, The Development of Chinese Agriculture 1950-1959. Urbana, Ill. The University of Illinois Press, 1969.
  A comprehensive study of Chinese agrarian policies and the social changes they catalyzed in the 1950's.

Tung Ta-lin. Agricultural Co-operation in China, Peking: Foreign Languages Press, 1959.
  Official accounts on policies and progress of collectivization in agriculture.

Walker, Kenneth R. Planning in Chinese Agriculture, Socialization and the Private Sector, 1956-1962, London: Frank Cass, 1965.
  An analysis of the Chinese attempt to promote agricultural development through socialist planning.

Walker, Kenneth R. "Collectivization in Retrospect: The Socialist High Tide of Autumn 1955-Spring 1956", The China Quarterly, April-June, 1966, pp. 1-43.
  A study of the critical period of China's agricultural collectivization by examining the social-political and economic atmosphere during that period.

Hou, Chi-ming. "Sources of Agricultural Growth in Communist China", The Journal of Asian Studies, Vol. XXVII, No. 4, Aug. 1968, pp. 721-737.
  A study attempts to examine and identify the factors responsible for the increase in agricultural output in the 1950's.

6.   Public Finance, Domestic and Foreign Trade

Cheng, Chu-yuan. Economic Relations Between Peking and Moscow, 1949-63, New York: Praeger, 1964.
  A survey of four major aspects of the economic relations between China and the Soviet Union including trade, technical aid, loans, and economic aid.

Cheng, Chu-yuan. Monetary Affairs of Communist China, Hong Kong, Union Research Institute, 1954.
  A survey of monetary management and the banking system.

Ecklund, George N. Financing the Chinese Government Budget, Chicago: Aldine, 1966.
  A discussion (based on official Chinese budgetary data) of revenue and tax policies used to support economic development during the First Five-Year Plan period.

Eckstein, Alexander. Communist China's Economic Growth and Foreign Trade, New York, McGraw-Hill, 1966.
  An authoritative analysis of Chinese development strategy, the pattern of growth, and trade relations with the Soviet Union, Eastern Europe and the rest of the world.

Chen Nai-Ruenn, "The Theory of Price Formation in Communist China", The China Quarterly, July-Sept. 1966, pp. 33-53.
  A survey of the debates on price formation among Chinese economists between 1953 and 1963.

72

Hsia, Ronald. Price Control in Communist China, New York: Institute of Pacific Relations, 1953.
A brief disucssion on the principles and mechanism of price control in the early years of Communist China.

Kwang, Ching-wen. "The Budgetary System of the People's Republic of China: A Preliminary Survey", Public Finance, No. 4, 1963, pp. 253-286.
An analysis of the budgetary process at various levels of government structure.

Galenson, Walter. "Economic Relations Between the Soviet Union and Communist China", in Nicolas Spulber (ed.), Study of the Soviet Economy, Bloomington: Indiana University, 1961, pp. 32-56.
An exposition on the effect of Soviet economic aid on economic development.

Hoeffding, Oleg. Sino-Soviet Economic Relations in Recent Years, Santa Monica, California: The Rand Corporation, 1960.
A survey of economic relations between China and the USSR in the late 1950's.

Lewin, Pauline. The Foreign Trade of Communist China, New York: Praeger, 1964.
A discussion of Chinese foreign trade during 1949 to 1962.

Perkins, D. H. Market Control and Planning in Communist China, Cambridge: Harvard University Press, 1966.
A standard work analyzing the role the market has played in the allocation of the labor force and in the distribution of consumers' goods.

King, Frank H. H. Money and Monetary Policy in China, Cambridge: Harvard University Press, 1965.
A systematic exposition of the structure of China's nineteenth century monetary system.

Young, Arthur N. China's Wartime Finance and Inflation, 1937-1945, Cambridge: Harvard University Press, 1965.
A comprehensive description and analysis of China's financial affairs during the war against Japan.

Vladimirov Iu. V. "The Question of Soviet-Chinese Economic Relations in 1950-1966", Chinese Economic Studies, Vol. 3, No. 1 Fall 1969, pp. 3-32, (translated from Problems of History No. 6, 1969).
    The most detailed account on many major problems concerning Sino-Soviet economic relations in the 1950's and 1960's by a Soviet official source.

7. Income and Standard of Living

Cheng, Chu-yuan. Income and Standard of Living in Mainland China, Hong Kong: Union Research Institute, 1957, 2 vols.
    A technical study on the composition of income, purchasing power, living standard of rural and urban population in Communist China in the 1950's.

Eckstein, Alexander. The National Income of Communist China, New York: Free Press of Glencoe, 1961.
    A detailed estimate of China's national income for the year 1952.

Hollister, William W. China's Gross National Product and Social Accounts, 1950-1957, Glencoe, Ill.: The Free Press, 1958.
    The first study on Communist China's national income and capital formation which employs the concepts used by the U. S. Department of Commerce.

Liu Ta-chung. China's National Income, 1931-36: An Exploratory Study, Washington, D. C.: The Brookings Institution, 1946.
    A well-compiled estimate which is based on less extensive data.

Liu Ta-chung and K. C. Yeh. The Economy of the Chinese Mainland: National Income and Economic Development, 1933-1959, Princeton, N. J.: Princeton University Press, 1965.
    The most authoritative and detailed study of China's national income in the 1933-59 period.

Ou, Pao-san. "A New Estimate of China's National Income", Journal of Political Economy, Vol. LIV, No. 6, Dec. 1946, pp. 547-554.
    A summary of the author's national income estimates for the pre-war China. The best available estimates for that period.

Ishikawa, Shigeru. National Income and Capital Formation in Mainland China, Tokyo: The Institute of Asian Economic Affairs, 1965.
    A study designed to clarify concepts and definitions of official Chinese data on national income rather than to present an independent estimate.

Schran, Peter. The Structure of Income in Communist China, unpublished Ph. D. thesis, University of California, Berkeley, 1961.

U. S. Government, Central Intelligence Agency. Average Annual Money Earnings of Workers and Staff in Communist China, Washington, D. C.: Government Printing Office, 1960.
    A brief technical study on the level and structure of money earnings during the 1950's.

8. Economic Planning

Chao Kuo-chun. Economic Planning and Organization in Mainland China, A Documentary Study (1949-1957), 2 vols., Cambridge: Harvard University Press, 1959 and 1960.
    A useful reference including major official documents on economic planning during the 1950's.

Chang, Y. N. "Industrial Administration in Communist China", Western Political Quarterly, Dec. 1956, pp. 850-872.
    A study of the organizational pattern and the political process by which policies relating to industrialization are made and controls are exercised.

Eckstein, Alexander. "Industrialization in a Hurry--Plans and Problems", The New Republic, Vol. 136, No. 19 (May 13, 1957), pp. 26-29.
    A discussion on the First Five-Year Plan.

Hooton, G. L. V. "The Planning Structure and the Five-Year Plan in China", Contemporary China, Vol. 1. University of Hong Kong, 1955, pp. 92-105.

Hsia, Ronald. Economic Planning in Communist China, New York: Institute of Pacific Relations, 1955.
A review of the planning mechanism during the First Five-Year Plan.

Kirby, E. Stuart. "The Central Structure of Economic Planning in Communist China", Far Eastern Economic Review, Vol. XXII, No. 24 (June 13, 1957) pp. 737-741 and Vol. XXII, No. 26 (July 27, 1957) pp. 754-765.
A detailed description of the function and organization of the state Planning Commission and the state Economic Commission in the State Council of Communist China.

Sate Planning Commission, People's Republic of China. The First Five-Year Plan for the Development of the National Economy, Peking: Foreign Language Press, 1956.
Official version of the First Five-Year Plan.

"China's Second Five-Year Plan", Far Eastern Economic Review, Vol. XXI, No. 16 (Oct. 18, 1956) pp. 489-90.
A brief account of the second Five-Year Plan.

K. W. "China's Third Five-Year Plan", China Quarterly, Jan. - March, 1966, pp. 171-75.
A brief analysis of China's Third FYP which was originally scheduled to begin early in 1963 but was delayed until 1966.

Li Choh-ming. "China's Industrial Development, 1958-1963", China Quarterly, Jan-March 1964, pp. 3-38.
A critical study of China's economic development plan.

Schurmann, H. F. "Organizational Contrasts Between Communist China and the Soviet Union", in Unity and Contradiction, by Kurt London (ed.), New York: Praeger, 1962, pp. 65-99.
A comparison of the structure and operation of industrial organizations between China and the USSR.

Wu, Yuan-li. "Planning, Management, and Economic Development in Communist China", in An Economic Profile of Mainland China, Vol. 1, pp. 97-120.

A review of national economic plan and its formulation and implementation, the sources of discrepancy between plan and reality, the indicated behavior of Chinese planners, and planning in the Chinese developmental model.

Kwang, Ching-wen. "The Economic Accounting System of State Enterprises in Mainland China", The International Journal of Accounting, Vol. 1, No. 2, 1966, pp. 61-99.

A detailed description of the procedure in preparing and implementing economic accounting in Chinese state enterprises.

9. Major Statistical Works

A. Evaluation of Official Statistics

Chao, Kang. "The Reliability of Industrial Output Data in Communist China", Journal of Asian Studies, Vol. XXII, No. 1 (Nov. 1962), pp. 47-65.

An examination of the pitfalls in official economic statistics.

Cheng, Chu-yuan. "A Note on Communist China's Statistical Data", in Communist China's Economy, 1949-62, pp. 181-190.

A survey of the changing quality of official statistical data from 1949 to 1960.

Durand, John D. "The Population Statistics of China A. D. 2-1953", Population Studies, Vol. XII, No. 3, (March, 1960), pp. 209-256.

An examination of historical data concerning the growth of population in China.

Klein, Sidney. "A Note on Statistical Techniques in Communist China", American Statistician, Oct. 1959.

Li Choh-ming, The Statistical System of Communist China, Berkeley and Los Angeles: University of California Press, 1962.

The first systematic study on Communist China's statistical system, its organization, operation and changes in statistical standard in different periods.

Taeuber, I. B. and L. A. Orleans, "A Note on the Population Statistics of Communist China", Population Index, Vol. 22, 1956, pp. 274-276.

A critical review of Chinese official population data.

Yoshio Akino. "Japanese Appraisal of Index Numbers of Industrial Production in Communist China", in JPRS, No. 12,037 (Jan. 19, 1962), pp. 59-67.

B. Sources of Official Statistics

Chen, Nai-Ruenn. Chinese Economic Statistics, Chicago: Aldine, 1967.

A voluminous compilation including most of the major statistical data available between 1949 and 1960. This work is of extreme value to those who cannot use original Chinese materials.

State Statistical Bureau, People's Republic of China. Ten Great Years, Peking: Foreign Language Press, 1960.

This volume is the most important official sourcebook for statistical data concerning economic and cultural achievements during the first decade of Communist control.

Yin, Hellen and Yi-chang Yin. Economic Statistics of Mainland China (1949-1957), Cambridge: Harvard University Press, 1960.

A useful compilation of official statistical data in the early years.

10. Major Periodicals on Chinese Economy

Far Eastern Economic Review, Hong Kong: 1946-.
 Published weekly, including interpretive articles and statistical reports on current economic conditions on mainland China. It is particularly strong in trade reports.

China Quarterly, London: 1960-.
 Published quarterly, the first major scholarly journal on Chinese affairs which includes occasionally major contributions on the Chinese economy, particularly industrial development.

China Reconstructs, Peking: 1952-.
 The Peking government's official propaganda journal on economic development; published monthly.

United Nations, Economic Commission for Asia and the Far East, Economic Survey of Asia and the Far East, 1947-.
 An annual publication which includes statistical and interpretive reports on current economic conditions in both mainland China and Taiwan.

Chinese Economic Studies, White Plains, New York.
 A translation of significant articles published originally in mainland China. Published quarterly.

Peking Review, Peking: 1958-.
 The Peking government's official propaganda weekly on every aspect of mainland China. It occasionally carries information on Chinese economic achievements.

Asian Survey, Berkeley, Calif.: 1961-.
 Published monthly, occasionally carrying articles on economic development in mainland China.

Journal of Asian Studies, Ann Arbor: 1946-.
 Published by the Association for Asian Studies, bimonthly, occasionally carrying important studies on the Chinese economy.

Current Scene, Hong Kong: 1962-.
Published by the U. S. Consulate General in Hong Kong, biweekly. It often carries analysis on the current economic situation in mainland China.

China News Analysis, Hong Kong: 1953-.
An excellent weekly newsletter on major development in Chinese mainland including many penetrating analyses on economic affairs.

Current Background, Hong Kong: 1949-. Mimeographed translations of important materials originally published in Chinese by the U. S. Consulate General in Hong Kong.

Selections from China Mainland Magazines (SCMM), Hong Kong: 1949-.
Mimeographed translations of important materials originally published in Chinese by the U. S. Consulate General in Hong Kong.

Survey of the Chinese Mainland Press (SCMP), Hong Kong, 1949-.
Mimeographed translations of news appearing in Mainland newspapers by the U. S. Consulate General in Hong Kong.

Union Research Services, Hong Kong: 1953-.
A semi-weekly translations published by the Union Research Institute in Hong Kong.

New China News Agency (NCNA),
Official English translation of Chinese Communist press, issued daily in Peking and London.

MICHIGAN PAPERS IN CHINESE STUDIES

No. 1, "The Chinese Economy, 1912-1949" by Albert Feuerwerker.

No. 2, "The Cultural Revolution: 1967 in Review" four essays by
Michel Oksenberg, Carl Riskin, Robert Scalapino, and Ezra Vogel.

No. 3, "Two Studies in Chinese Literature": 'One Aspect of Form in
the Arias of Yüan Opera' by Dale Johnson; and "Hsü K'o's Huang Shan
Travel Diaries' translated by Li Chi, with an introduction, commentary,
notes, and bibliography by Chang Chun-shu.

No. 4, "Early Communist China: Two Studies": 'The Fu-t'ien Incident'
by Ronald Suleski; and 'Agrarian Reform in Kwangtung, 1950-1953' by
Daniel Bays.

No. 5, "The Chinese Economy, ca. 1870-1911" by Albert Feuerwerker.

No. 6, "Chinese Paintings in Chinese Publications, 1956-1968: An
Annotated Bibliography and An Index to the Paintings", by E. J. Laing.

No. 7, "The Treaty Ports and China's Modernization: What Went
Wrong?" by Rhoads Murphey.

No. 8, "Two Twelfth Century Texts on Chinese Painting": Shan-shui
ch'un-ch'üan chi by Han Cho and Chapters Nine and Ten of Hua-chi
by Teng Ch'un translated by Robert J. Maeda.

Price: $2.00 (US) each
(Price for Special Issue No. 6: $3.50 (US))

Available from:

Center for Chinese Studies
The University of Michigan
Lane Hall
Ann Arbor, Michigan 48104
United States of America

MICHIGAN ABSTRACTS OF CHINESE AND
JAPANESE WORKS ON CHINESE HISTORY

No. 1, "The Ming Tribute Grain System" by Hoshi Ayao, translated
by Mark Elvin.

No. 2, "Commerce and Society in Sung China" by Shiba Yoshinobu,
translated by Mark Elvin.

Price: $2. 50 (US) each

Available from:

Center for Chinese Studies
The University of Michigan
Lane Hall
Ann Arbor, Michigan 48104
United States of America

Printed and bound by CPI Group (UK) Ltd, Croydon, CR0 4YY

13/04/2025

14656528-0005